PYTHYON CODE WARRIOR

WARRIOR

Working with DAO

By Richard Thomas Edwards

CONTENTS

WELCOME TO DAO

The Godfather of Data Access

I CONSIDER DAO – which means Data Access Objects -TO BE THE GODFATHER OF DATA ACCESS BECAUSE IT HAS BEEN THE WAY TO CONNECT TO AND CREATE DATABASES, TABLES AND STORED PROCEEDURES YEARS BEFORE I WENT TO WORK FOR MICROSOFT.

In fact, knowing it helped me to land my first job at Microsoft.

But there was something coming through the development pipeline that made every attempt of dethroning it: Active X Data Objects.

Their reasoning was quite simple, Do the same thing in memory and it will be much faster.

Well, that worked until hard drives – SSDs and the newest kid on the block, USB SSDs – no longer made the speed distinction a factor and, once again, DAO is back in the spotlight.

LET'S VENTURE BACKWARDS IN TIME FOR JUST A MOMENT

Anyone who remembers the wild, wild Microsoft days knows what the worlds DLL HELL meant. Those were the good old days, right?

R.I.P to them!

Anyway, back then we had things like DAO.DBEngine.25 –AKA the thunker – which served to support the notion that 16-bit and 32-bit versions of data access. It was Microsoft's way of appeasing the gods. And, of course that was short lived when

Microsoft grew up fast and started compromising quality support for higher profit margins.

So, by 1998, DAO.DBEngine.35, a 32-bit only Database Engine had been created and most us working in Technical Support were pretty sure ADO was going to replace it.

It didn't. In fact, when VB6 came out with DAO.DBEngine.36, we very quickly learned why.

In fact, I wrote two KB Articles on the issue. Then installation and the remove of Access 97 removed the key in the registry that made the VB6 development environment effectively useless with respect to DAO.

So, after that fiasco, most of us were pretty sure DAO was on the way out.

We were, once again, wrong.

Office 2007 shipped with DAO.DBEngine.120.

BACK TO THE FUTURE

Today, after installing Office 365, I find no changes in the COM version of DAO. The COM version supports dbVersion120. However, the .Net version of COM supports up to dbVersion150 according to the Object Browser. I'm not even sure that is possible considering the same functionality found in the .Net COM version should be the same.

For right now, none of this really matters as we need to focus on connecting to DAO and what you can do with what you have installed.

WHAT DAO CAN DO FOR YOU

First, DAO supports local as well as remote connections.

Second, you can connect to a database using:

There are ISAMS -- Indexed Sequential Access Method – well as all the ODBC – Open Database Connectivity – drivers including SQL Server that can be used along with the standard connectivity using database naming. Below are some examples of what is meant:

Please keep in mind that you could use DAO.DBEngine.35, DAO.DBEngine.36 or DAO.DBEngine.120 with all the below examples.

```
import win32com.client
import string


Dim Filename
Filename = "C:\Program Files (x86)\Microsoft Visual Studio\VB98\Nwind.mdb"
DBEngine = win32com.client.Dispatch ("DAO.DBEngine.36")
db = DBEngine.OpenDatabase(filename)
```

A ISAM CONNECTION USING DAO

It works like this:

```
Filename = "C:\ISAMS\Text"
DBEngine = win32com.client.Dispatch ("DAO.DBEngine.36")
db = DBEngine.OpenDatabase(filename,,, "Text; hdr=yes;")
```

And the Query:
```
rs = db.OpenRecordset("Select * from [Myfile.csv]")
```

TO CREATE A DAO DATABASE

```
dbLangGeneral = ";LANGID=0x0409;CP=1252;COUNTRY=0"

dbVersion30 = 32
dbVersion40 = 64
dbVersion120 = 128

dbEngine = win32com.client.Dispatch ("DAO.DBEngine.120")
Set db = dbEngine.CreateDatabase("C:\MyFirst.accdb", dbLangGeneral, dbVersion120)
```

```
Set dbEngine = win32com.client.Dispatch ("DAO.DBEngine.36")
Set   db   =   dbEngine.CreateDatabase("C:\MyFirst.mdb",   dbLangGeneral,
dbVersion40)

Set dbEngine = win32com.client.Dispatch ("DAO.DBEngine.35")
Set   db   =   dbEngine.CreateDatabase("C:\MyFirst.mdb",   dbLangGeneral,
dbVersion30)
```

TO OPEN THE DATABASE

```
dbEngine = win32com.client.Dispatch ("DAO.DBEngine.120")
db = dbEngine.OpenDatabase("C:\MyFirst.accdb")

dbEngine = win32com.client.Dispatch ("DAO.DBEngine.36")
db = dbEngine.OpenDatabase("C:\MyFirst.mdb")

dbEngine = win32com.client.Dispatch ("DAO.DBEngine.35")
db = dbEngine.OpenDatabase("C:\MyFirst.mdb")
```

CREATE AND POPULATE TABLE

```
tbldef = db.CreateTableDef("Process_Properties")
for x in range(rs1.Fields.Count):
    fld = tbldef.CreateField(Prop.Name, 12)
    fld.AllowZeroLength = true
    tbldef.Fields.Append(fld)

db.TableDefs.Append(tbldef)
```

I use 12 or a memo field because I don't want to have to worry about the data type or the size of the information I'm passing in. This could become problematic if I didn't.

```
rs = db.OpenRecordset("Processes_Properties")
while rs1.EOF == False:
    rs.AddNew()
    for x in range(rs1.Fields.Count):
        rs.Fields[x].Value = str(rs1.Fields[x].Value)

    rs.Update()
```

```
rs1.MoveFirst()
```

OPEN RECORDSET

```
rs = db.OpenRecordset("Select * From Processes_Properties",
Exclusive:=False)
```

Or:

```
rs = db.OpenRecordset("Processes_Properties")
```

ASP CODE

THERE IS NOTHING FANTASIC ABOUT CREATING ASP OR ASPX WEB PAGES. In fact, additional hoops must be jumped – web site where you can cut and paste what you just created from here is one of them. So, with that said, I've added enough bells and whistles into the code structure to make it worth your while.

Here's what is in store for you:

- Report View
  - Horizontal
    - None
    - Button
    - Combobox
    - Div
    - Link
    - Listbox
    - Span
    - Textarea
    - Textbox
  - Vertical
    - None
    - Button
    - Combobox
    - Div
    - Link
    - Listbox
    - Span
    - Textarea
    - Textbox

- Table View
  - Horizontal
    - None
    - Button
    - Combobox

- Div
- Link
- Listbox
- Span
- Textarea
- Textbox
  - Vertical
    - None
    - Button
    - Combobox
    - Div
    - Link
    - Listbox
    - Span
    - Textarea
    - Textbox

```
import win32com.client
import string

ws = win32com.client.Dispatch("WScript.Shell")
fso = win32com.client.Dispatch("Scripting.FileSystemObject")
txtstream = fso.OpenTextFile(ws.CurrentDirectory + "\Products.asp", 2, True, -2)
txtstream.WriteLine("<html>")
txtstream.WriteLine("<head>")
txtstream.WriteLine("<title>" + Tablename + "</title>")
#Add Stylesheet here
txtstream.WriteLine("<body>")
txtstream.WriteLine("</br>")
```

HORIZONTAL REPORTS

```
txtstream.WriteLine("<table border=0 cellspacing=3 cellpadding=3>")
txtstream.WriteLine("<%")
txtstream.WriteLine("Response.Write(""<tr>"" + vbcrlf)")
for x = 0 in rs.fields.count:
    txtstream.WriteLine("Response.Write(""<th    style=""    font-family:Calibri,
Sans-Serif;font-size:  12px;color:darkred;""   align='left'  nowrap='nowrap'>"  +
rs.Fields(x).Name + "</th>"" + vbcrlf)")

    txtstream.WriteLine("Response.Write(""</tr>"" + vbcrlf)")

while rs.eof = false:
    txtstream.WriteLine("Response.Write(""<tr>"" + vbcrlf)")
    for x = 0 in rs.fields.count:
```

NONE

```
        txtstream.WriteLine("Response.Write(""<td   style=""font-family:Calibri,
Sans-Serif;font-size:   12px;color:navy;""    align='left'   nowrap='nowrap'>"   +
rs.Fields(x).Value + "</td>"" + vbcrlf)")
```

Button

```
txtstream.WriteLine("Response.Write("""<td   style="""font-family:Calibri,
Sans-Serif;font-size:    12px;color:navy;"""    align='left'    nowrap='true'><button
style='width:100%;' value ='" + rs.Fields(x).Value + "'>" + rs.Fields(x).Value +
"</button></td>""" + vbcrlf)")
```

COMBOBOX

```
txtstream.WriteLine("Response.Write("""<td   style="""font-family:Calibri,
Sans-Serif;font-size: 12px;color:navy;""" align='left' nowrap='true'><select><option
value    =    """    +    rs.Fields(x).Value    +    """>"    +    rs.Fields(x).Value    +
"</option></select></td>""" + vbcrlf)")
```

DIV

```
txtstream.WriteLine("Response.Write("""<td   style="""font-family:Calibri,
Sans-Serif;font-size:   12px;color:navy;"""   align='left'   nowrap='true'><div>"   +
rs.Fields(x).Value + "</div></td>""" + vbcrlf)")
```

LINK

```
txtstream.WriteLine("Response.Write("""<td   style="""font-family:Calibri,
Sans-Serif;font-size: 12px;color:navy;""" align='left' nowrap='true'><a href='" +
rs.Fields(x).Value + "'>" + rs.Fields(x).Value + "</a></td>""" + vbcrlf)")
```

LISTBOX

```
txtstream.WriteLine("Response.Write("""<td   style="""font-family:Calibri,
Sans-Serif;font-size:    12px;color:navy;"""    align='left'    nowrap='true'><select
multiple><option value = """ + rs.Fields(x).Value + """>" + rs.Fields(x).Value +
"</option></select></td>""" + vbcrlf)")
```

SPAN

```
txtstream.WriteLine("Response.Write("""<td   style="""font-family:Calibri,
Sans-Serif;font-size:   12px;color:navy;"""   align='left'   nowrap='true'><span>"   +
rs.Fields(x).Value + "</span></td>""" + vbcrlf)")
```

TEXTAREA

```
txtstream.WriteLine("Response.Write("""<td   style="""font-family:Calibri,
Sans-Serif;font-size: 12px;color:navy;""" align='left' nowrap='true'><textarea>" +
rs.Fields(x).Value + "</textarea></td>""" + vbcrlf)")
```

TEXTBOX

```
            txtstream.WriteLine("Response.Write(""<td   style=""font-family:Calibri,
Sans-Serif;font-size:   12px;color:navy;""   align='left'   nowrap='true'><input
type=text value=""" + rs.Fields(x).Value + """></input></td>"" + vbcrlf)")

        txtstream.WriteLine("Response.Write(""</tr>"" + vbcrlf)")
        rs.MoveNext

    txtstream.WriteLine("%>")
    txtstream.WriteLine("</table>")
    txtstream.WriteLine("</body>")
    txtstream.WriteLine("</html>")
    txtstream.Close()
```

VERTICAL REPORTS

```
    txtstream.WriteLine("<table border=0 cellspacing=3 cellpadding=3>")
    txtstream.WriteLine("<%")
    for x = 0 in rs.fields.count:
        txtstream.WriteLine("Response.Write(""<tr><th         style=""      font-
family:Calibri,     Sans-Serif;font-size:     12px;color:darkred;""      align='left'
nowrap='nowrap'>" + rs.Fields(x).Name + "</th>"" + vbcrlf)")
        rs.MoveFirst()
        while rs.eof = false:
         txtstream.WriteLine("Response.Write(""<td    style=""font-family:Calibri,
Sans-Serif;font-size: 12px;color:navy;"">"  +  rs.Fields(x).Value  +  "</td>""  +
vbcrlf)")
```

NONE

```
            txtstream.WriteLine("Response.Write(""<td  style=""font-family:Calibri,
Sans-Serif;font-size:   12px;color:navy;""   align='left'   nowrap='nowrap'>"   +
rs.Fields(x).Value + "</td>"" + vbcrlf)")
```

Button

```
        txtstream.WriteLine("Response.Write(""<td    style=""font-family:Calibri,
Sans-Serif;font-size:   12px;color:navy;""   align='left'   nowrap='true'><button
style='width:100%;' value ='" + rs.Fields(x).Value + "'>" + rs.Fields(x).Value +
"</button></td>"" + vbcrlf)")
```

Combobox

```
txtstream.WriteLine("Response.Write(""<td     style=""font-family:Calibri,
Sans-Serif;font-size: 12px;color:navy;"" align='left' nowrap='true'><select><option
value   =   """   +   rs.Fields(x).Value   +   """>"   +   rs.Fields(x).Value   +
"</option></select></td>"" + vbcrlf)")
```

Div

```
txtstream.WriteLine("Response.Write(""<td      style=""font-family:Calibri,
Sans-Serif;font-size:  12px;color:navy;""  align='left'  nowrap='true'><div>"  +
rs.Fields(x).Value + "</div></td>"" + vbcrlf)")
```

Link

```
txtstream.WriteLine("Response.Write(""<td style=""font-family:Calibri, Sans-
Serif;font-size:  12px;color:navy;""  align='left'  nowrap='true'><a  href='"  +
rs.Fields(x).Value + "'>" + rs.Fields(x).Value + "</a></td>"" + vbcrlf)")
```

Listbox

```
txtstream.WriteLine("Response.Write(""<td style=""font-family:Calibri, Sans-
Serif;font-size:    12px;color:navy;""    align='left'    nowrap='true'><select
multiple><option value = """ + rs.Fields(x).Value + """>" + rs.Fields(x).Value +
"</option></select></td>"" + vbcrlf)")
```

Span

```
txtstream.WriteLine("Response.Write(""<td      style=""font-family:Calibri,
Sans-Serif;font-size: 12px;color:navy;"" align='left' nowrap='true'><span>" +
rs.Fields(x).Value + "</span></td>"" + vbcrlf)")
```

Textarea

```
txtstream.WriteLine("Response.Write(""<td style=""font-family:Calibri, Sans-
Serif;font-size:  12px;color:navy;""  align='left'  nowrap='true'><textarea>"  +
rs.Fields(x).Value + "</textarea></td>"" + vbcrlf)")
```

Textbox

```
txtstream.WriteLine("Response.Write(""<td     style=""font-family:Calibri,
Sans-Serif;font-size:  12px;color:navy;""  align='left'  nowrap='true'><input
type=text value=""" + rs.Fields(x).Value + """></input></td>"" + vbcrlf)")
```

```
        rs.MoveNext

    txtstream.WriteLine("Response.Write(""</tr>"" + vbcrlf)")

txtstream.WriteLine("%>")
txtstream.WriteLine("</table>")
txtstream.WriteLine("</body>")
txtstream.WriteLine("</html>")
txtstream.Close()
```

```
    txtstream.WriteLine("<table        style='border:Double;border-width:1px;border-
color:navy;' rules=all frames=both cellpadding=2 cellspacing=2 Width=0>")
    txtstream.WriteLine("<%")
    txtstream.WriteLine("Response.Write(""<tr>"" + vbcrlf)")
    for x = 0 in rs.fields.count:
        txtstream.WriteLine("Response.Write(""<th    style=""   font-family:Calibri,
Sans-Serif;font-size:  12px;color:darkred;""   align='left'  nowrap='nowrap'>" +
rs.Fields(x).Name + "</th>"" + vbcrlf)")

    while rs.eof = false:
      txtstream.WriteLine("Response.Write(""<tr>"" + vbcrlf)")
        for x = 0 in rs.fields.count:
```

```
            txtstream.WriteLine("Response.Write(""<td   style=""font-family:Calibri,
Sans-Serif;font-size:  12px;color:navy;""   align='left'  nowrap='nowrap'>" +
rs.Fields(x).Value + "</td>"" + vbcrlf)")
```

```
            txtstream.WriteLine("Response.Write(""<td   style=""font-family:Calibri,
Sans-Serif;font-size:  12px;color:navy;""   align='left'  nowrap='true'><button
style='width:100%;' value ='" + rs.Fields(x).Value + "'>" + rs.Fields(x).Value +
"</button></td>"" + vbcrlf)")
```

```
        txtstream.WriteLine("Response.Write(""<td   style=""font-family:Calibri,
Sans-Serif;font-size: 12px;color:navy;"" align='left' nowrap='true'><select><option
value    =    """   +   rs.Fields(x).Value   +   """>"   +   rs.Fields(x).Value   +
"</option></select></td>"" + vbcrlf)")
```

DIV

```
        txtstream.WriteLine("Response.Write(""<td   style=""font-family:Calibri,
Sans-Serif;font-size:  12px;color:navy;""  align='left'  nowrap='true'><div>"  +
rs.Fields(x).Value + "</div></td>"" + vbcrlf)")
```

LINK

```
        txtstream.WriteLine("Response.Write(""<td   style=""font-family:Calibri,
Sans-Serif;font-size: 12px;color:navy;"" align='left' nowrap='true'><a href='" +
rs.Fields(x).Value + "'>" + rs.Fields(x).Value + "</a></td>"" + vbcrlf)")
```

LISTBOX

```
        txtstream.WriteLine("Response.Write(""<td   style=""font-family:Calibri,
Sans-Serif;font-size:  12px;color:navy;""   align='left'   nowrap='true'><select
multiple><option value = """ + rs.Fields(x).Value + """>" + rs.Fields(x).Value +
"</option></select></td>"" + vbcrlf)")
```

SPAN

```
        txtstream.WriteLine("Response.Write(""<td   style=""font-family:Calibri,
Sans-Serif;font-size:  12px;color:navy;""  align='left'  nowrap='true'><span>"  +
rs.Fields(x).Value + "</span></td>"" + vbcrlf)")
```

TEXTAREA

```
        txtstream.WriteLine("Response.Write(""<td   style=""font-family:Calibri,
Sans-Serif;font-size: 12px;color:navy;"" align='left' nowrap='true'><textarea>" +
rs.Fields(x).Value + "</textarea></td>"" + vbcrlf)")
```

TEXTBOX

```
        txtstream.WriteLine("Response.Write(""<td   style=""font-family:Calibri,
Sans-Serif;font-size:   12px;color:navy;""    align='left'    nowrap='true'><input
type=text value=""" + rs.Fields(x).Value + """></input></td>"" + vbcrlf)")

    txtstream.WriteLine("Response.Write(""</tr>"" + vbcrlf)")
    rs.MoveNext
```

```
txtstream.WriteLine("%>")
txtstream.WriteLine("</table>")
txtstream.WriteLine("</body>")
txtstream.WriteLine("</html>")
txtstream.Close()
```

VERTICAL TABLES

```
txtstream.WriteLine("<table        style='border:Double;border-width:1px;border-
color:navy;' rules=all frames=both cellpadding=2 cellspacing=2 Width=0>")

txtstream.WriteLine("<%")

for x = 0 in rs.fields.count:
        txtstream.WriteLine("Response.Write(""<tr><th        style=""        font-
family:Calibri,      Sans-Serif;font-size:      12px;color:darkred;""      align='left'
nowrap='nowrap'>" + rs.Fields(x).Name + "</th>"" + vbcrlf)")
        rs.MoveFirst()
        while rs.eof == False:
         txtstream.WriteLine("Response.Write(""<td    style=""font-family:Calibri,
Sans-Serif;font-size:   12px;color:navy;"">"   +   rs.Fields(x).Value   +   "</td>""   +
vbcrlf)")
```

NONE

```
          txtstream.WriteLine("Response.Write(""<td  style=""font-family:Calibri,
Sans-Serif;font-size:   12px;color:navy;""   align='left'   nowrap='nowrap'>"   +
rs.Fields(x).Value + "</td>"" + vbcrlf)")
```

Button

```
        txtstream.WriteLine("Response.Write(""<td    style=""font-family:Calibri,
Sans-Serif;font-size:   12px;color:navy;""   align='left'   nowrap='true'><button
style='width:100%;' value ='" + rs.Fields(x).Value + "'>" + rs.Fields(x).Value +
"</button></td>"" + vbcrlf)")
```

Combobox

```
        txtstream.WriteLine("Response.Write(""<td    style=""font-family:Calibri,
Sans-Serif;font-size: 12px;color:navy;"" align='left' nowrap='true'><select><option
value   =   """   +   rs.Fields(x).Value   +   """>"   +   rs.Fields(x).Value   +
"</option></select></td>"" + vbcrlf)")
```

Div

```
        txtstream.WriteLine("Response.Write(""<td    style=""font-family:Calibri,
Sans-Serif;font-size: 12px;color:navy;"" align='left' nowrap='true'><div>" +
rs.Fields(x).Value + "</div></td>"" + vbcrlf)")
```

Link

```
        txtstream.WriteLine("Response.Write(""<td style=""font-family:Calibri, Sans-
Serif;font-size: 12px;color:navy;"" align='left' nowrap='true'><a href='" +
rs.Fields(x).Value + "'>" + rs.Fields(x).Value + "</a></td>"" + vbcrlf)")
```

Listbox

```
        txtstream.WriteLine("Response.Write(""<td style=""font-family:Calibri, Sans-
Serif;font-size:   12px;color:navy;""    align='left'    nowrap='true'><select
multiple><option value = """ + rs.Fields(x).Value + """>" + rs.Fields(x).Value +
"</option></select></td>"" + vbcrlf)")
```

Span

```
        txtstream.WriteLine("Response.Write(""<td    style=""font-family:Calibri,
Sans-Serif;font-size: 12px;color:navy;"" align='left' nowrap='true'><span>" +
rs.Fields(x).Value + "</span></td>"" + vbcrlf)")
```

Textarea

```
        txtstream.WriteLine("Response.Write(""<td style=""font-family:Calibri, Sans-
Serif;font-size: 12px;color:navy;"" align='left' nowrap='true'><textarea>" +
rs.Fields(x).Value + "</textarea></td>"" + vbcrlf)")
```

Textbox

```
        txtstream.WriteLine("Response.Write(""<td    style=""font-family:Calibri,
Sans-Serif;font-size:   12px;color:navy;""    align='left'    nowrap='true'><input
type=text value=""" + rs.Fields(x).Value + """></input></td>"" + vbcrlf)")
        rs.MoveNext
```

```
        txtstream.WriteLine("Response.Write(""</tr>"" + vbcrlf)")

txtstream.WriteLine("%>")
txtstream.WriteLine("</table>")
txtstream.WriteLine("</body>")
txtstream.WriteLine("</html>")
txtstream.Close()
```

ASPX CODE

```
import win32com.client
import string

ws = win32com.client.Dispatch("WScript.Shell")
fso = win32com.client.Dispatch("Scripting.FileSystemObject")
txtstream = fso.OpenTextFile(ws.CurrentDirectory + "\Products.asp", 2, True, -2)
txtstream.WriteLine("<html>")
txtstream.WriteLine("<head>")
txtstream.WriteLine("<title>" + Tablename + "</title>")
#Add Stylesheet here
txtstream.WriteLine("<body>")
txtstream.WriteLine("</br>")
```

```
txtstream.WriteLine("<table border=0 cellspacing=3 cellpadding=3>")
txtstream.WriteLine("<%")
txtstream.WriteLine("Response.Write("""<tr>""" + vbcrlf)")
for x = 0 in rs.fields.count:
    txtstream.WriteLine("Response.Write("""<th    style=""    font-family:Calibri,
Sans-Serif;font-size:  12px;color:darkred;"""   align='left'  nowrap='nowrap'>" +
rs.Fields(x).Name + "</th>""" + vbcrlf)")

txtstream.WriteLine("Response.Write("""</tr>""" + vbcrlf)")

while rs.eof = false:
    txtstream.WriteLine("Response.Write("""<tr>""" + vbcrlf)")
    for x = 0 in rs.fields.count:
```

```
            txtstream.WriteLine("Response.Write(""<td   style=""font-family:Calibri,
Sans-Serif;font-size:   12px;color:navy;""   align='left'   nowrap='nowrap'>"   +
rs.Fields(x).Value + "</td>""" + vbcrlf)")
```

Button

```
            txtstream.WriteLine("Response.Write(""<td   style=""font-family:Calibri,
Sans-Serif;font-size:   12px;color:navy;""   align='left'   nowrap='true'><button
style='width:100%;' value ='" + rs.Fields(x).Value + "'>" + rs.Fields(x).Value +
"</button></td>""" + vbcrlf)")
```

COMBOBOX

```
            txtstream.WriteLine("Response.Write(""<td   style=""font-family:Calibri,
Sans-Serif;font-size: 12px;color:navy;"" align='left' nowrap='true'><select><option
value   =   """   +   rs.Fields(x).Value   +   """>"   +   rs.Fields(x).Value   +
"</option></select></td>""" + vbcrlf)")
```

DIV

```
            txtstream.WriteLine("Response.Write(""<td   style=""font-family:Calibri,
Sans-Serif;font-size:   12px;color:navy;""   align='left'   nowrap='true'><div>"   +
rs.Fields(x).Value + "</div></td>""" + vbcrlf)")
```

LINK

```
            txtstream.WriteLine("Response.Write(""<td   style=""font-family:Calibri,
Sans-Serif;font-size: 12px;color:navy;"" align='left' nowrap='true'><a href='" +
rs.Fields(x).Value + "'>" + rs.Fields(x).Value + "</a></td>""" + vbcrlf)")
```

LISTBOX

```
            txtstream.WriteLine("Response.Write(""<td   style=""font-family:Calibri,
Sans-Serif;font-size:   12px;color:navy;""   align='left'   nowrap='true'><select
multiple><option value = """ + rs.Fields(x).Value + """>" + rs.Fields(x).Value +
"</option></select></td>""" + vbcrlf)")
```

SPAN

```
            txtstream.WriteLine("Response.Write(""<td   style=""font-family:Calibri,
Sans-Serif;font-size:   12px;color:navy;""   align='left'   nowrap='true'><span>"   +
rs.Fields(x).Value + "</span></td>""" + vbcrlf)")
```

```
        txtstream.WriteLine("Response.Write(""<td   style=""font-family:Calibri,
Sans-Serif;font-size: 12px;color:navy;"" align='left' nowrap='true'><textarea>" +
rs.Fields(x).Value + "</textarea></td>""" + vbcrlf)")
```

```
        txtstream.WriteLine("Response.Write(""<td   style=""font-family:Calibri,
Sans-Serif;font-size:   12px;color:navy;""    align='left'    nowrap='true'><input
type=text value=""" + rs.Fields(x).Value + """></input></td>""" + vbcrlf)")

    txtstream.WriteLine("Response.Write(""</tr>""" + vbcrlf)")
    rs.MoveNext

txtstream.WriteLine("%>")
txtstream.WriteLine("</table>")
txtstream.WriteLine("</body>")
txtstream.WriteLine("</html>")
txtstream.Close()
```

VERTICAL REPORTS

```
txtstream.WriteLine("<table border=0 cellspacing=3 cellpadding=3>")
txtstream.WriteLine("<%")
for x = 0 in rs.fields.count:
        txtstream.WriteLine("Response.Write(""<tr><th        style=""       font-
family:Calibri,    Sans-Serif;font-size:    12px;color:darkred;""      align='left'
nowrap='nowrap'>" + rs.Fields(x).Name + "</th>""" + vbcrlf)")
        rs.MoveFirst()
        while rs.eof = false:
        txtstream.WriteLine("Response.Write(""<td    style=""font-family:Calibri,
Sans-Serif;font-size: 12px;color:navy;"">" + rs.Fields(x).Value + "</td>""" +
vbcrlf)")
```

```
        txtstream.WriteLine("Response.Write(""<td style=""font-family:Calibri,
Sans-Serif;font-size:   12px;color:navy;""    align='left'    nowrap='nowrap'>"   +
rs.Fields(x).Value + "</td>""" + vbcrlf)")
```

Button

```
        txtstream.WriteLine("Response.Write(""<td     style=""font-family:Calibri,
Sans-Serif;font-size:   12px;color:navy;""     align='left'   nowrap='true'><button
style='width:100%;' value ='" + rs.Fields(x).Value + "'>" + rs.Fields(x).Value +
"</button></td>"" + vbcrlf)")
```

Combobox

```
        txtstream.WriteLine("Response.Write(""<td     style=""font-family:Calibri,
Sans-Serif;font-size: 12px;color:navy;"" align='left' nowrap='true'><select><option
value   =   """   +   rs.Fields(x).Value   +   """>"   +   rs.Fields(x).Value   +
"</option></select></td>"" + vbcrlf)")
```

Div

```
     txtstream.WriteLine("Response.Write(""<td      style=""font-family:Calibri,
Sans-Serif;font-size:   12px;color:navy;""    align='left'   nowrap='true'><div>"   +
rs.Fields(x).Value + "</div></td>"" + vbcrlf)")
```

Link

```
   txtstream.WriteLine("Response.Write(""<td style=""font-family:Calibri, Sans-
Serif;font-size:   12px;color:navy;""    align='left'   nowrap='true'><a   href='"   +
rs.Fields(x).Value + "'>" + rs.Fields(x).Value + "</a></td>"" + vbcrlf)")
```

Listbox

```
   txtstream.WriteLine("Response.Write(""<td style=""font-family:Calibri, Sans-
Serif;font-size:    12px;color:navy;""     align='left'     nowrap='true'><select
multiple><option value = """ + rs.Fields(x).Value + """>" + rs.Fields(x).Value +
"</option></select></td>"" + vbcrlf)")
```

Span

```
        txtstream.WriteLine("Response.Write(""<td      style=""font-family:Calibri,
Sans-Serif;font-size: 12px;color:navy;"" align='left' nowrap='true'><span>" +
rs.Fields(x).Value + "</span></td>"" + vbcrlf)")
```

Textarea

```
        txtstream.WriteLine("Response.Write(""<td style="""font-family:Calibri, Sans-
Serif;font-size:  12px;color:navy;"""  align='left'  nowrap='true'><textarea>"  +
rs.Fields(x).Value + "</textarea></td>""" + vbcrlf)")
```

Textbox

```
          txtstream.WriteLine("Response.Write(""<td    style="""font-family:Calibri,
Sans-Serif;font-size:   12px;color:navy;"""   align='left'   nowrap='true'><input
type=text value="""" + rs.Fields(x).Value + """"></input></td>""" + vbcrlf)")
          rs.MoveNext

      txtstream.WriteLine("Response.Write(""</tr>""" + vbcrlf)")

  txtstream.WriteLine("%>")
  txtstream.WriteLine("</table>")
  txtstream.WriteLine("</body>")
  txtstream.WriteLine("</html>")
  txtstream.Close()
```

HORIZONTAL TABLES

```
  txtstream.WriteLine("<table        style='border:Double;border-width:1px;border-
color:navy;' rules=all frames=both cellpadding=2 cellspacing=2 Width=0>")
  txtstream.WriteLine("<%")
  txtstream.WriteLine("Response.Write(""<tr>""" + vbcrlf)")
  for x = 0 in rs.fields.count:
      txtstream.WriteLine("Response.Write(""<th    style="""   font-family:Calibri,
Sans-Serif;font-size:  12px;color:darkred;"""   align='left'   nowrap='nowrap'>"  +
rs.Fields(x).Name + "</th>""" + vbcrlf)")


  while rs.eof = false:
    txtstream.WriteLine("Response.Write(""<tr>""" + vbcrlf)")
      for x = 0 in rs.fields.count:
```

NONE

```vbnet
        txtstream.WriteLine("Response.Write(""<td   style=""font-family:Calibri,
Sans-Serif;font-size:   12px;color:navy;""   align='left'   nowrap='nowrap'>"   +
rs.Fields(x).Value + "</td>""" + vbcrlf)")
```

```vbnet
        txtstream.WriteLine("Response.Write(""<td   style=""font-family:Calibri,
Sans-Serif;font-size:   12px;color:navy;""   align='left'   nowrap='true'><button
style='width:100%;' value ='" + rs.Fields(x).Value + "'>" + rs.Fields(x).Value +
"</button></td>""" + vbcrlf)")
```

```vbnet
        txtstream.WriteLine("Response.Write(""<td   style=""font-family:Calibri,
Sans-Serif;font-size: 12px;color:navy;"" align='left' nowrap='true'><select><option
value   =   """   +   rs.Fields(x).Value   +   """>"   +   rs.Fields(x).Value   +
"</option></select></td>""" + vbcrlf)")
```

```vbnet
        txtstream.WriteLine("Response.Write(""<td   style=""font-family:Calibri,
Sans-Serif;font-size:   12px;color:navy;""   align='left'   nowrap='true'><div>"   +
rs.Fields(x).Value + "</div></td>""" + vbcrlf)")
```

```vbnet
        txtstream.WriteLine("Response.Write(""<td   style=""font-family:Calibri,
Sans-Serif;font-size: 12px;color:navy;"" align='left' nowrap='true'><a href='" +
rs.Fields(x).Value + "'>" + rs.Fields(x).Value + "</a></td>""" + vbcrlf)")
```

```vbnet
        txtstream.WriteLine("Response.Write(""<td   style=""font-family:Calibri,
Sans-Serif;font-size:   12px;color:navy;""   align='left'   nowrap='true'><select
multiple><option value = """ + rs.Fields(x).Value + """>" + rs.Fields(x).Value +
"</option></select></td>""" + vbcrlf)")
```

```vbnet
        txtstream.WriteLine("Response.Write(""<td   style=""font-family:Calibri,
Sans-Serif;font-size:   12px;color:navy;""   align='left'   nowrap='true'><span>"   +
rs.Fields(x).Value + "</span></td>""" + vbcrlf)")
```

```
        txtstream.WriteLine("Response.Write(""<td   style=""font-family:Calibri,
Sans-Serif;font-size: 12px;color:navy;"" align='left' nowrap='true'><textarea>" +
rs.Fields(x).Value + "</textarea></td>"" + vbcrlf)")
```

```
        txtstream.WriteLine("Response.Write(""<td   style=""font-family:Calibri,
Sans-Serif;font-size:   12px;color:navy;""   align='left'   nowrap='true'><input
type=text value=""" + rs.Fields(x).Value + """></input></td>"" + vbcrlf)")

        txtstream.WriteLine("Response.Write(""</tr>"" + vbcrlf)")
        rs.MoveNext

    txtstream.WriteLine("%>")
    txtstream.WriteLine("</table>")
    txtstream.WriteLine("</body>")
    txtstream.WriteLine("</html>")
    txtstream.Close()
```

VERTICAL TABLES

```
    txtstream.WriteLine("<table        style='border:Double;border-width:1px;border-
color:navy;' rules=all frames=both cellpadding=2 cellspacing=2 Width=0>")

    txtstream.WriteLine("<%")

    for x = 0 in rs.fields.count:
        txtstream.WriteLine("Response.Write(""<tr><th         style=""       font-
family:Calibri,    Sans-Serif;font-size:    12px;color:darkred;""        align='left'
nowrap='nowrap'>" + rs.Fields(x).Name + "</th>"" + vbcrlf)")
        rs.MoveFirst()
        while rs.eof == False:
        txtstream.WriteLine("Response.Write(""<td    style=""font-family:Calibri,
Sans-Serif;font-size: 12px;color:navy;"">" + rs.Fields(x).Value + "</td>"" +
vbcrlf)")
```

txtstream.WriteLine("Response.Write(""<td style=""font-family:Calibri, Sans-Serif;font-size: 12px;color:navy;"" align='left' nowrap='nowrap'>" + rs.Fields(x).Value + "</td>"" + vbcrlf)")

Button

txtstream.WriteLine("Response.Write(""<td style=""font-family:Calibri, Sans-Serif;font-size: 12px;color:navy;"" align='left' nowrap='true'><button style='width:100%;' value ='" + rs.Fields(x).Value + "'>" + rs.Fields(x).Value + "</button></td>"" + vbcrlf)")

Combobox

txtstream.WriteLine("Response.Write(""<td style=""font-family:Calibri, Sans-Serif;font-size: 12px;color:navy;"" align='left' nowrap='true'><select><option value = """" + rs.Fields(x).Value + """">" + rs.Fields(x).Value + "</option></select></td>"" + vbcrlf)")

Div

txtstream.WriteLine("Response.Write(""<td style=""font-family:Calibri, Sans-Serif;font-size: 12px;color:navy;"" align='left' nowrap='true'> " + rs.Fields(x).Value + " </td>"" + vbcrlf)")

Link

txtstream.WriteLine("Response.Write(""<td style=""font-family:Calibri, Sans-Serif;font-size: 12px;color:navy;"" align='left' nowrap='true'><a href='" + rs.Fields(x).Value + "'>" + rs.Fields(x).Value + "</a></td>"" + vbcrlf)")

Listbox

txtstream.WriteLine("Response.Write(""<td style=""font-family:Calibri, Sans-Serif;font-size: 12px;color:navy;"" align='left' nowrap='true'><select multiple><option value = """" + rs.Fields(x).Value + """">" + rs.Fields(x).Value + "</option></select></td>"" + vbcrlf)")

Span

txtstream.WriteLine("Response.Write(""<td style=""font-family:Calibri, Sans-Serif;font-size: 12px;color:navy;"" align='left' nowrap='true'>" + rs.Fields(x).Value + "</td>"" + vbcrlf)")

Textarea

```
    txtstream.WriteLine("Response.Write(""<td style=""font-family:Calibri, Sans-Serif;font-size:  12px;color:navy;""  align='left'  nowrap='true'><textarea>"  + rs.Fields(x).Value + "</textarea></td>"" + vbcrlf)")
```

Textbox

```
        txtstream.WriteLine("Response.Write(""<td  style=""font-family:Calibri, Sans-Serif;font-size:  12px;color:navy;""  align='left'  nowrap='true'><input type=text value=""" + rs.Fields(x).Value + """></input></td>"" + vbcrlf)")
        rs.MoveNext

        txtstream.WriteLine("Response.Write(""</tr>"" + vbcrlf)")

    txtstream.WriteLine("%>")
    txtstream.WriteLine("</table>")
    txtstream.WriteLine("</body>")
    txtstream.WriteLine("</html>")
    txtstream.Close()
```

HTA CODE

LIKE ASP AND ASPX, HTA BEEN AROUND FOR SOME TIME NOW. Despite the fact the concept appears to be old or outdated You should know that it is still being used as HTML as an EXE.

```
ws = win32com.client.Dispatch("WScript.Shell")
fso = win32com.client.Dispatch("Scripting.FileSystemObject")
txtstream = fso.OpenTextFile(ws.CurrentDirectory + "\Products.hta", 2, True, -2)
txtstream.WriteLine("<html>")
txtstream.WriteLine("<head>")
txtstream.WriteLine("<HTA:APPLICATION ")
txtstream.WriteLine("ID = ""Products"" ")
txtstream.WriteLine("APPLICATIONNAME = ""Products"" ")
txtstream.WriteLine("SCROLL = ""yes"" ")
txtstream.WriteLine("SINGLEINSTANCE = ""yes"" ")
txtstream.WriteLine("WINDOWSTATE = ""maximize"" >")
txtstream.WriteLine("<title>" + Tablename + "</title>")
#Add Stylesheet here
txtstream.WriteLine("<body>")
txtstream.WriteLine("</br>")
```

HORIZONTAL REPORTS

```
txtstream.WriteLine("<table border=0 cellspacing=3 cellpadding=3>")
txtstream.WriteLine("<tr>")
for x = 0 in rs.fields.count:
```

```
        txtstream.WriteLine("<th style="" font-family:Calibri, Sans-Serif;font-size:
12px;color:darkred;"" align='left' nowrap='nowrap'>" + rs.Fields(x).Name +
"</th>")

    txtstream.WriteLine("</tr>")

    while rs.eof = false:
      txtstream.WriteLine("<tr>")
      for x = 0 in rs.fields.count:
```

NONE

```
        txtstream.WriteLine("<td style=""font-family:Calibri, Sans-Serif;font-
size: 12px;color:navy;"" align='left' nowrap='nowrap'>" + rs.Fields(x).Value +
"</td>")
```

Button

```
        txtstream.WriteLine("<td style=""font-family:Calibri, Sans-Serif;font-
size: 12px;color:navy;"" align='left' nowrap='true'><button style='width:100%;'
value ='" + rs.Fields(x).Value + "'>" + rs.Fields(x).Value + "</button></td>")
```

COMBOBOX

```
        txtstream.WriteLine("<td style=""font-family:Calibri, Sans-Serif;font-
size: 12px;color:navy;"" align='left' nowrap='true'><select><option value = """ +
rs.Fields(x).Value + """>" + rs.Fields(x).Value + "</option></select></td>")
```

DIV

```
        txtstream.WriteLine("<td style=""font-family:Calibri, Sans-Serif;font-
size: 12px;color:navy;"" align='left' nowrap='true'><div>" + rs.Fields(x).Value +
"</div></td>")
```

LINK

```
        txtstream.WriteLine("<td style=""font-family:Calibri, Sans-Serif;font-
size: 12px;color:navy;"" align='left' nowrap='true'><a href='" + rs.Fields(x).Value +
"'>" + rs.Fields(x).Value + "</a></td>")
```

LISTBOX

```
        txtstream.WriteLine("<td   style=""font-family:Calibri,   Sans-Serif;font-
size: 12px;color:navy;"" align='left' nowrap='true'><select multiple><option value =
""" + rs.Fields(x).Value + """>" + rs.Fields(x).Value + "</option></select></td>")
```

```
        txtstream.WriteLine("<td   style=""font-family:Calibri,   Sans-Serif;font-
size: 12px;color:navy;"" align='left' nowrap='true'><span>" + rs.Fields(x).Value +
"</span></td>")
```

```
        txtstream.WriteLine("<td   style=""font-family:Calibri,   Sans-Serif;font-
size: 12px;color:navy;"" align='left' nowrap='true'><textarea>" + rs.Fields(x).Value
+ "</textarea></td>")
```

```
        txtstream.WriteLine("<td   style=""font-family:Calibri,   Sans-Serif;font-
size: 12px;color:navy;"" align='left' nowrap='true'><input type=text value=""" +
rs.Fields(x).Value + """></input></td>")
```

```
    txtstream.WriteLine("</tr>")
    rs.MoveNext

txtstream.WriteLine("</table>")
txtstream.WriteLine("</body>")
txtstream.WriteLine("</html>")
txtstream.Close()
```

```
txtstream.WriteLine("<table border=0 cellspacing=3 cellpadding=3>")
for x = 0 in rs.fields.count:
        txtstream.WriteLine("<tr><th       style=""    font-family:Calibri,    Sans-
Serif;font-size:    12px;color:darkred;""    align='left'   nowrap='nowrap'>"    +
rs.Fields(x).Name + "</th>")
        rs.MoveFirst()
        while rs.eof = false:
```

txtstream.WriteLine("<td style=""font-family:Calibri, Sans-Serif;font-size: 12px;color:navy;"">" + rs.Fields(x).Value + "</td>")

txtstream.WriteLine("<td style=""font-family:Calibri, Sans-Serif;font-size: 12px;color:navy;"" align='left' nowrap='nowrap'>" + rs.Fields(x).Value + "</td>")

Button

txtstream.WriteLine("<td style=""font-family:Calibri, Sans-Serif;font-size: 12px;color:navy;"" align='left' nowrap='true'><button style='width:100%;' value ='" + rs.Fields(x).Value + "'>" + rs.Fields(x).Value + "</button></td>")

Combobox

txtstream.WriteLine("<td style=""font-family:Calibri, Sans-Serif;font-size: 12px;color:navy;"" align='left' nowrap='true'><select><option value = """ + rs.Fields(x).Value + """>" + rs.Fields(x).Value + "</option></select></td>")

Div

txtstream.WriteLine("<td style=""font-family:Calibri, Sans-Serif;font-size: 12px;color:navy;"" align='left' nowrap='true'> " + rs.Fields(x).Value + " </td>")

Link

txtstream.WriteLine("<td style=""font-family:Calibri, Sans-Serif;font-size: 12px;color:navy;"" align='left' nowrap='true'><a href='" + rs.Fields(x).Value + "'>" + rs.Fields(x).Value + "</a></td>")

Listbox

txtstream.WriteLine("<td style=""font-family:Calibri, Sans-Serif;font-size: 12px;color:navy;"" align='left' nowrap='true'><select multiple><option value = """ + rs.Fields(x).Value + """>" + rs.Fields(x).Value + "</option></select></td>")

Span

txtstream.WriteLine("<td style=""font-family:Calibri, Sans-Serif;font-size: 12px;color:navy;"" align='left' nowrap='true'>" + rs.Fields(x).Value + "</td>")

```
    txtstream.WriteLine("<td    style=""font-family:Calibri,    Sans-Serif;font-size:
12px;color:navy;""  align='left'  nowrap='true'><textarea>" + rs.Fields(x).Value +
"</textarea></td>")
```

```
        txtstream.WriteLine("<td    style=""font-family:Calibri,    Sans-Serif;font-
size: 12px;color:navy;""  align='left'  nowrap='true'><input  type=text  value=""" +
rs.Fields(x).Value + """></input></td>")
        rs.MoveNext

    txtstream.WriteLine("</tr>")

  txtstream.WriteLine("</table>")
  txtstream.WriteLine("</body>")
  txtstream.WriteLine("</html>")
  txtstream.Close()
```

HORIZONTAL TABLES

```
    txtstream.WriteLine("<table        style='border:Double;border-width:1px;border-
color:navy;' rules=all frames=both cellpadding=2 cellspacing=2 Width=0>")
    txtstream.WriteLine("<tr>")
    for x = 0 in rs.fields.count:
      txtstream.WriteLine("<th  style=""  font-family:Calibri,  Sans-Serif;font-size:
12px;color:darkred;""   align='left'   nowrap='nowrap'>"   +   rs.Fields(x).Name   +
"</th>")


    while rs.eof = false:
      txtstream.WriteLine("<tr>")
        for x = 0 in rs.fields.count:
```

txtstream.WriteLine("<td style="""font-family:Calibri, Sans-Serif;font-size: 12px;color:navy;""" align='left' nowrap='nowrap'>" + rs.Fields(x).Value + "</td>")

Button

txtstream.WriteLine("<td style="""font-family:Calibri, Sans-Serif;font-size: 12px;color:navy;""" align='left' nowrap='true'><button style='width:100%;' value ='" + rs.Fields(x).Value + "'>" + rs.Fields(x).Value + "</button></td>")

COMBOBOX

txtstream.WriteLine("<td style="""font-family:Calibri, Sans-Serif;font-size: 12px;color:navy;""" align='left' nowrap='true'><select><option value = """" + rs.Fields(x).Value + """">" + rs.Fields(x).Value + "</option></select></td>")

DIV

txtstream.WriteLine("<td style="""font-family:Calibri, Sans-Serif;font-size: 12px;color:navy;""" align='left' nowrap='true'> " + rs.Fields(x).Value + " </td>")

LINK

txtstream.WriteLine("<td style="""font-family:Calibri, Sans-Serif;font-size: 12px;color:navy;""" align='left' nowrap='true'><a href='" + rs.Fields(x).Value + "'>" + rs.Fields(x).Value + "</a></td>")

LISTBOX

txtstream.WriteLine("<td style="""font-family:Calibri, Sans-Serif;font-size: 12px;color:navy;""" align='left' nowrap='true'><select multiple><option value = """" + rs.Fields(x).Value + """">" + rs.Fields(x).Value + "</option></select></td>")

SPAN

txtstream.WriteLine("<td style="""font-family:Calibri, Sans-Serif;font-size: 12px;color:navy;""" align='left' nowrap='true'>" + rs.Fields(x).Value + "</td>")

TEXTAREA

```
                txtstream.WriteLine("<td   style=""font-family:Calibri,  Sans-Serif;font-
size: 12px;color:navy;"" align='left' nowrap='true'><textarea>" + rs.Fields(x).Value
+ "</textarea></td>")
```

```
                txtstream.WriteLine("<td   style=""font-family:Calibri,  Sans-Serif;font-
size: 12px;color:navy;"" align='left' nowrap='true'><input type=text value=""" +
rs.Fields(x).Value + """></input></td>")

            txtstream.WriteLine("</tr>")
            rs.MoveNext

        txtstream.WriteLine("</table>")
        txtstream.WriteLine("</body>")
        txtstream.WriteLine("</html>")
        txtstream.Close()
```

VERTICAL TABLES

```
        txtstream.WriteLine("<table        style='border:Double;border-width:1px;border-
color:navy;' rules=all frames=both cellpadding=2 cellspacing=2 Width=0>")
        for x = 0 in rs.fields.count:
                txtstream.WriteLine("<tr><th        style=""    font-family:Calibri,    Sans-
Serif;font-size:    12px;color:darkred;""    align='left'    nowrap='nowrap'>"    +
rs.Fields(x).Name + "</th>")
                rs.MoveFirst()
                while rs.eof == False:
                txtstream.WriteLine("<td   style=""font-family:Calibri,  Sans-Serif;font-
size: 12px;color:navy;"">" + rs.Fields(x).Value + "</td>")
```

```
                txtstream.WriteLine("<td   style=""font-family:Calibri,  Sans-Serif;font-
size:  12px;color:navy;""  align='left'  nowrap='nowrap'>"  +  rs.Fields(x).Value  +
"</td>")
```

```
            txtstream.WriteLine("<td    style="""font-family:Calibri,    Sans-Serif;font-
size: 12px;color:navy;"""  align='left'  nowrap='true'><button  style='width:100%;'
value ='" + rs.Fields(x).Value + "'>" + rs.Fields(x).Value + "</button></td>")
```

Combobox

```
            txtstream.WriteLine("<td    style="""font-family:Calibri,    Sans-Serif;font-
size: 12px;color:navy;"""  align='left'  nowrap='true'><select><option value = """" +
rs.Fields(x).Value + """">" + rs.Fields(x).Value + "</option></select></td>")
```

Div

```
        txtstream.WriteLine("<td  style="""font-family:Calibri,  Sans-Serif;font-size:
12px;color:navy;"""   align='left'   nowrap='true'><div>"   +   rs.Fields(x).Value   +
"</div></td>")
```

Link

```
      txtstream.WriteLine("<td   style="""font-family:Calibri,   Sans-Serif;font-size:
12px;color:navy;""" align='left' nowrap='true'><a href='" + rs.Fields(x).Value + "'>"
+ rs.Fields(x).Value + "</a></td>")
```

Listbox

```
      txtstream.WriteLine("<td   style="""font-family:Calibri,   Sans-Serif;font-size:
12px;color:navy;""" align='left' nowrap='true'><select multiple><option value = """"
+ rs.Fields(x).Value + """">" + rs.Fields(x).Value + "</option></select></td>")
```

Span

```
        txtstream.WriteLine("<td style="""font-family:Calibri, Sans-Serif;font-size:
12px;color:navy;"""  align='left'  nowrap='true'><span>"  +  rs.Fields(x).Value  +
"</span></td>")
```

Textarea

```
      txtstream.WriteLine("<td   style="""font-family:Calibri,   Sans-Serif;font-size:
12px;color:navy;"""  align='left'  nowrap='true'><textarea>"  +  rs.Fields(x).Value  +
"</textarea></td>")
```

Textbox

```
        txtstream.WriteLine("<td    style=""font-family:Calibri,   Sans-Serif;font-
size: 12px;color:navy;""  align='left'  nowrap='true'><input type=text value=""" +
rs.Fields(x).Value + """></input></td>")
        rs.MoveNext

        txtstream.WriteLine("</tr>")

    txtstream.WriteLine("</table>")
    txtstream.WriteLine("</body>")
    txtstream.WriteLine("</html>")
    txtstream.Close()
```

HTML CODE

WHAT CAN I SAY ABOUT HTML5 AND CSS THAT HASN'T BEEN SAID ALREADY? Well, I can say that it has come a long way since the 1990s.

```
import win32com.client
import string

ws = win32com.client.Dispatch("WScript.Shell")
fso = win32com.client.Dispatch("Scripting.FileSystemObject")
txtstream = fso.OpenTextFile(ws.CurrentDirectory + "\Products.html", 2, True,
-2)
txtstream.WriteLine("<html>")
txtstream.WriteLine("<head>")
txtstream.WriteLine("<title>" + Tablename + "</title>")
#Add Stylesheet here
txtstream.WriteLine("<body>")
txtstream.WriteLine("</br>")
```

```
txtstream.WriteLine("<table border=0 cellspacing=3 cellpadding=3>")
txtstream.WriteLine("<tr>")
for x = 0 in rs.fields.count:
    txtstream.WriteLine("<th style="" font-family:Calibri, Sans-Serif;font-size:
12px;color:darkred;"" align='left' nowrap='nowrap'>" + rs.Fields(x).Name +
"</th>")
```

```
txtstream.WriteLine("</tr>")

while rs.eof = false:
    txtstream.WriteLine("<tr>")
    for x = 0 in rs.fields.count:
```

NONE

```
        txtstream.WriteLine("<td   style=""font-family:Calibri,   Sans-Serif;font-
size: 12px;color:navy;""   align='left'   nowrap='nowrap'>"   +   rs.Fields(x).Value   +
"</td>")
```

Button

```
        txtstream.WriteLine("<td   style=""font-family:Calibri,   Sans-Serif;font-
size:  12px;color:navy;""   align='left'   nowrap='true'><button   style='width:100%;'
value ='" + rs.Fields(x).Value + "'>" + rs.Fields(x).Value + "</button></td>")
```

COMBOBOX

```
        txtstream.WriteLine("<td   style=""font-family:Calibri,   Sans-Serif;font-
size: 12px;color:navy;"" align='left' nowrap='true'><select><option value = """ +
rs.Fields(x).Value + """>" + rs.Fields(x).Value + "</option></select></td>")
```

DIV

```
        txtstream.WriteLine("<td   style=""font-family:Calibri,   Sans-Serif;font-
size:  12px;color:navy;""   align='left'   nowrap='true'><div>"   +   rs.Fields(x).Value   +
"</div></td>")
```

LINK

```
        txtstream.WriteLine("<td   style=""font-family:Calibri,   Sans-Serif;font-
size: 12px;color:navy;"" align='left' nowrap='true'><a href='" + rs.Fields(x).Value +
"'>" + rs.Fields(x).Value + "</a></td>")
```

LISTBOX

```
            txtstream.WriteLine("<td    style="""font-family:Calibri,    Sans-Serif;font-
size: 12px;color:navy;"" align='left' nowrap='true'><select multiple><option value =
"""" + rs.Fields(x).Value + """">" + rs.Fields(x).Value + "</option></select></td>")
```

SPAN

```
            txtstream.WriteLine("<td    style="""font-family:Calibri,    Sans-Serif;font-
size: 12px;color:navy;"" align='left' nowrap='true'><span>" + rs.Fields(x).Value +
"</span></td>")
```

TEXTAREA

```
            txtstream.WriteLine("<td    style="""font-family:Calibri,    Sans-Serif;font-
size: 12px;color:navy;"" align='left' nowrap='true'><textarea>" + rs.Fields(x).Value
+ "</textarea></td>")
```

TEXTBOX

```
            txtstream.WriteLine("<td    style="""font-family:Calibri,    Sans-Serif;font-
size: 12px;color:navy;"" align='left' nowrap='true'><input type=text value="""" +
rs.Fields(x).Value + """"></input></td>")


        txtstream.WriteLine("</tr>")
        rs.MoveNext

    txtstream.WriteLine("</table>")
    txtstream.WriteLine("</body>")
    txtstream.WriteLine("</html>")
    txtstream.Close()
```

VERTICAL REPORTS

```
    txtstream.WriteLine("<table border=0 cellspacing=3 cellpadding=3>")
    for x = 0 in rs.fields.count:
        txtstream.WriteLine("<tr><th      style=""    font-family:Calibri,    Sans-
Serif;font-size:    12px;color:darkred;""    align='left'    nowrap='nowrap'>"    +
rs.Fields(x).Name + "</th>")
        rs.MoveFirst()
        while rs.eof = false:
```

txtstream.WriteLine("<td   style=""font-family:Calibri,   Sans-Serif;font-size: 12px;color:navy;"">" + rs.Fields(x).Value + "</td>")

NONE

txtstream.WriteLine("<td   style=""font-family:Calibri,   Sans-Serif;font-size: 12px;color:navy;"" align='left' nowrap='nowrap'>" + rs.Fields(x).Value + "</td>")

Button

txtstream.WriteLine("<td   style=""font-family:Calibri,   Sans-Serif;font-size: 12px;color:navy;"" align='left' nowrap='true'><button style='width:100%;' value ='" + rs.Fields(x).Value + "'>" + rs.Fields(x).Value + "</button></td>")

Combobox

txtstream.WriteLine("<td   style=""font-family:Calibri,   Sans-Serif;font-size: 12px;color:navy;"" align='left' nowrap='true'><select><option value = """ + rs.Fields(x).Value + """>" + rs.Fields(x).Value + "</option></select></td>")

Div

txtstream.WriteLine("<td style=""font-family:Calibri, Sans-Serif;font-size: 12px;color:navy;""   align='left'   nowrap='true'> "   +   rs.Fields(x).Value   + " </td>")

Link

txtstream.WriteLine("<td   style=""font-family:Calibri,   Sans-Serif;font-size: 12px;color:navy;"" align='left' nowrap='true'><a href='" + rs.Fields(x).Value + "'>" + rs.Fields(x).Value + "</a></td>")

Listbox

txtstream.WriteLine("<td   style=""font-family:Calibri,   Sans-Serif;font-size: 12px;color:navy;"" align='left' nowrap='true'><select multiple><option value = """ + rs.Fields(x).Value + """>" + rs.Fields(x).Value + "</option></select></td>")

Span

txtstream.WriteLine("<td style=""font-family:Calibri, Sans-Serif;font-size: 12px;color:navy;"" align='left' nowrap='true'>" + rs.Fields(x).Value + "</td>")

```
    txtstream.WriteLine("<td    style=""font-family:Calibri,    Sans-Serif;font-size:
12px;color:navy;""  align='left'  nowrap='true'><textarea>" + rs.Fields(x).Value +
"</textarea></td>")
```

```
        txtstream.WriteLine("<td    style=""font-family:Calibri,    Sans-Serif;font-
size: 12px;color:navy;""  align='left'  nowrap='true'><input  type=text  value=""" +
rs.Fields(x).Value + """></input></td>")
        rs.MoveNext

    txtstream.WriteLine("</tr>")

  txtstream.WriteLine("</table>")
  txtstream.WriteLine("</body>")
  txtstream.WriteLine("</html>")
  txtstream.Close()
```

HORIZONTAL TABLES

```
  txtstream.WriteLine("<table        style='border:Double;border-width:1px;border-
color:navy;' rules=all frames=both cellpadding=2 cellspacing=2 Width=0>")
  txtstream.WriteLine("<tr>")
  for x = 0 in rs.fields.count:
    txtstream.WriteLine("<th  style=""  font-family:Calibri,  Sans-Serif;font-size:
12px;color:darkred;""   align='left'   nowrap='nowrap'>"  +  rs.Fields(x).Name  +
"</th>")


  while rs.eof = false:
    txtstream.WriteLine("<tr>")
      for x = 0 in rs.fields.count:
```

txtstream.WriteLine("<td style=""font-family:Calibri, Sans-Serif;font-size: 12px;color:navy;"" align='left' nowrap='nowrap'>" + rs.Fields(x).Value + "</td>")

Button

txtstream.WriteLine("<td style=""font-family:Calibri, Sans-Serif;font-size: 12px;color:navy;"" align='left' nowrap='true'><button style='width:100%;' value ='" + rs.Fields(x).Value + "'>" + rs.Fields(x).Value + "</button></td>")

COMBOBOX

txtstream.WriteLine("<td style=""font-family:Calibri, Sans-Serif;font-size: 12px;color:navy;"" align='left' nowrap='true'><select><option value = """ + rs.Fields(x).Value + """>" + rs.Fields(x).Value + "</option></select></td>")

DIV

txtstream.WriteLine("<td style=""font-family:Calibri, Sans-Serif;font-size: 12px;color:navy;"" align='left' nowrap='true'> " + rs.Fields(x).Value + " </td>")

LINK

txtstream.WriteLine("<td style=""font-family:Calibri, Sans-Serif;font-size: 12px;color:navy;"" align='left' nowrap='true'><a href='" + rs.Fields(x).Value + "'>" + rs.Fields(x).Value + "</a></td>")

LISTBOX

txtstream.WriteLine("<td style=""font-family:Calibri, Sans-Serif;font-size: 12px;color:navy;"" align='left' nowrap='true'><select multiple><option value = """ + rs.Fields(x).Value + """>" + rs.Fields(x).Value + "</option></select></td>")

SPAN

txtstream.WriteLine("<td style=""font-family:Calibri, Sans-Serif;font-size: 12px;color:navy;"" align='left' nowrap='true'>" + rs.Fields(x).Value + "</td>")

TEXTAREA

```
        txtstream.WriteLine("<td   style=""font-family:Calibri,   Sans-Serif;font-
size: 12px;color:navy;"" align='left' nowrap='true'><textarea>" + rs.Fields(x).Value
+ "</textarea></td>")
```

TEXTBOX

```
        txtstream.WriteLine("<td   style=""font-family:Calibri,   Sans-Serif;font-
size: 12px;color:navy;"" align='left' nowrap='true'><input type=text value=""" +
rs.Fields(x).Value + """></input></td>")

      txtstream.WriteLine("</tr>")
      rs.MoveNext

   txtstream.WriteLine("</table>")
   txtstream.WriteLine("</body>")
   txtstream.WriteLine("</html>")
   txtstream.Close()
```

VERTICAL TABLES

```
   txtstream.WriteLine("<table       style='border:Double;border-width:1px;border-
color:navy;' rules=all frames=both cellpadding=2 cellspacing=2 Width=0>")
   for x = 0 in rs.fields.count:
      txtstream.WriteLine("<tr><th      style=""   font-family:Calibri,   Sans-
Serif;font-size:   12px;color:darkred;""   align='left'   nowrap='nowrap'>"   +
rs.Fields(x).Name + "</th>")
      rs.MoveFirst()
      while rs.eof == False:
       txtstream.WriteLine("<td   style=""font-family:Calibri,   Sans-Serif;font-
size: 12px;color:navy;"">" + rs.Fields(x).Value + "</td>")
```

NONE

```
        txtstream.WriteLine("<td   style=""font-family:Calibri,   Sans-Serif;font-
size:  12px;color:navy;""  align='left'  nowrap='nowrap'>"  +  rs.Fields(x).Value  +
"</td>")
```

Button

```
        txtstream.WriteLine("<td    style=""font-family:Calibri,    Sans-Serif;font-
size: 12px;color:navy;""  align='left'  nowrap='true'><button   style='width:100%;'
value ='" + rs.Fields(x).Value + "'>" + rs.Fields(x).Value + "</button></td>")
```

Combobox

```
        txtstream.WriteLine("<td    style=""font-family:Calibri,    Sans-Serif;font-
size: 12px;color:navy;""  align='left' nowrap='true'><select><option value = """ +
rs.Fields(x).Value + """>" + rs.Fields(x).Value + "</option></select></td>")
```

Div

```
      txtstream.WriteLine("<td  style=""font-family:Calibri,  Sans-Serif;font-size:
12px;color:navy;""    align='left'    nowrap='true'><div>"    +    rs.Fields(x).Value    +
"</div></td>")
```

Link

```
      txtstream.WriteLine("<td    style=""font-family:Calibri,    Sans-Serif;font-size:
12px;color:navy;"" align='left' nowrap='true'><a href='" + rs.Fields(x).Value + "'>"
+ rs.Fields(x).Value + "</a></td>")
```

Listbox

```
      txtstream.WriteLine("<td    style=""font-family:Calibri,    Sans-Serif;font-size:
12px;color:navy;"" align='left' nowrap='true'><select multiple><option value = """
+ rs.Fields(x).Value + """>" + rs.Fields(x).Value + "</option></select></td>")
```

Span

```
        txtstream.WriteLine("<td style=""font-family:Calibri, Sans-Serif;font-size:
12px;color:navy;""    align='left'    nowrap='true'><span>"    +    rs.Fields(x).Value    +
"</span></td>")
```

Textarea

```
      txtstream.WriteLine("<td    style=""font-family:Calibri,    Sans-Serif;font-size:
12px;color:navy;""    align='left'    nowrap='true'><textarea>"    +    rs.Fields(x).Value    +
"</textarea></td>")
```

Textbox

```
        txtstream.WriteLine("<td    style=""font-family:Calibri,   Sans-Serif;font-
size: 12px;color:navy;""  align='left'  nowrap='true'><input  type=text  value=""" +
rs.Fields(x).Value + """></input></td>")
        rs.MoveNext

        txtstream.WriteLine("</tr>")

    txtstream.WriteLine("</table>")
    txtstream.WriteLine("</body>")
    txtstream.WriteLine("</html>")
    txtstream.Close()
```

DELIMITED FILES

Chapter Subtitle

*Chapter Epigraph uses a quote or verse to
introduce the chapter and set the stage.
—Attribute the quote*

THERE ARE MANY DIFFERENT KINDS OF DELIMITED FILES. The ones we are going to be using are the most common ones. And by Common, this will include:

- Colon Delimited
- Comma Delimited
- Exclamation Delimited
- Semi-Colon Delimited
- Tab Delimited
- Tilde Delimited

Essentially, the only differences in the code is how the delimiter is used, but the code examples are also going to show you how the information can be arranged in both Horizontal and Vertical Views.

```
ws = win32com.client.Dispatch("WScript.Shell")
fso = win32com.client.Dispatch("Scripting.FileSystemObject")
txtstream = fso.OpenTextFile(ws.CurrentDirectory + "\Products.txt", 2, True, -
2)
    tstr= ""
Horizontal
    for x = 0 in rs.fields.count:
        if tstr <> "":
            tstr = tstr + ":"

        tstr = tstr + rs.Fields(x).Name

    txtstream.Writeline(tstr)
    tstr = ""
    rs.MoveFirst()
    while rs.eof = false:
        for x = 0 in rs.fields.count:
            if tstr <> "":
                tstr = tstr + ":"

            tstr = tstr + '"' + rs.Fields(x).Value + '"'

        txtstream.Writeline(tstr)
        tstr = ""
        rs.MoveNext
```

```
    for x = 0 in rs.fields.count:
        tstr = rs.Fields(x).Name
        rs.MoveFirst()
        while rs.eof = false:
            if tstr <> "":
                tstr = tstr + ":"
```

```
        tstr = tstr + '"' + rs.Fields(x).Value + '"'
        rs.MoveNext

    txtstream.Writeline(tstr)
    tstr = ""

    txtstream.Close
```

```
    ws = win32com.client.Dispatch("WScript.Shell")
    fso = win32com.client.Dispatch("Scripting.FileSystemObject")
    txtstream = fso.OpenTextFile(ws.CurrentDirectory + "\Products.csv", 2, True,
-2)
    tstr= ""
Horizontal
for x = 0 in rs.fields.count:
    if tstr <> "":
        tstr = tstr + ","

    tstr = tstr + rs.Fields(x).Name

txtstream.Writeline(tstr)
tstr = ""
rs.MoveFirst()
while rs.eof = false:
    for x = 0 in rs.fields.count:
        if tstr <> "":
            tstr = tstr + ","

        tstr = tstr + '"' + rs.Fields(x).Value + '"'

    txtstream.Writeline(tstr)
    tstr = ""
    rs.MoveNext
```

```
for x = 0 in rs.fields.count:
    tstr = rs.Fields(x).Name
    rs.MoveFirst()
    while rs.eof = false:
        if tstr <> "":
            tstr = tstr + ","

        tstr = tstr + '"' + rs.Fields(x).Value + '"'
        rs.MoveNext

    txtstream.Writeline(tstr)
    tstr = ""


    txtstream.Close
```

```
ws = win32com.client.Dispatch("WScript.Shell")
fso = win32com.client.Dispatch("Scripting.FileSystemObject")
txtstream = fso.OpenTextFile(ws.CurrentDirectory + "\Products.txt", 2, True, -
2)
    tstr= ""
Horizontal
    for x = 0 in rs.fields.count:
        if tstr <> "":
            tstr = tstr + "!"

        tstr = tstr + rs.Fields(x).Name

    txtstream.Writeline(tstr)
```

```
tstr = ""
rs.MoveFirst()
while rs.eof = false:
    for x = 0 in rs.fields.count:
        if tstr <> "":
            tstr = tstr + "!"

        tstr = tstr + '"' + rs.Fields(x).Value + '"'

    txtstream.Writeline(tstr)
    tstr = ""
    rs.MoveNext
```

EXCLAMATION DELIMITED VERTICAL

```
for x = 0 in rs.fields.count:
    tstr = rs.Fields(x).Name
    rs.MoveFirst()
    while rs.eof = false:
        if tstr <> "":
            tstr = tstr + "!"

        tstr = tstr + '"' + rs.Fields(x).Value + '"'
        rs.MoveNext

    txtstream.Writeline(tstr)
    tstr = ""


    txtstream.Close
```

SEMI COLON DELIMITED HORIZONTAL

```
ws = win32com.client.Dispatch("WScript.Shell")
fso = win32com.client.Dispatch("Scripting.FileSystemObject")
txtstream = fso.OpenTextFile(ws.CurrentDirectory + "\Products.txt", 2, True, -
2)
```

```
tstr= ""
```
Horizontal
```
   for x = 0 in rs.fields.count:
      if tstr <> "":
         tstr = tstr + ";"

      tstr = tstr + rs.Fields(x).Name

   txtstream.Writeline(tstr)
   tstr = ""
   rs.MoveFirst()
   while rs.eof = false:
      for x = 0 in rs.fields.count:
         if tstr <> "":
            tstr = tstr + ";"

         tstr = tstr + '"' + rs.Fields(x).Value + '"'

      txtstream.Writeline(tstr)
      tstr = ""
      rs.MoveNext
```

SEMI COLON DELIMITED VERTICAL

```
   for x = 0 in rs.fields.count:
      tstr = rs.Fields(x).Name
      rs.MoveFirst()
      while rs.eof = false:
         if tstr <> "":
            tstr = tstr + ";"

         tstr = tstr + '"' + rs.Fields(x).Value + '"'
         rs.MoveNext

      txtstream.Writeline(tstr)
      tstr = ""
```

```
        txtstream.Close
```

TAB DELIMITED HORIZONTAL

```
    ws = win32com.client.Dispatch("WScript.Shell")
    fso = win32com.client.Dispatch("Scripting.FileSystemObject")
    txtstream = fso.OpenTextFile(ws.CurrentDirectory + "\Products.txt", 2, True, -
2)
    tstr= ""

    for x = 0 in rs.fields.count:
      if tstr <> "":
         tstr = tstr + vbtab

      tstr = tstr + rs.Fields(x).Name

    txtstream.Writeline(tstr)
    tstr = ""
    rs.MoveFirst()
    while rs.eof = false:
      for x = 0 in rs.fields.count:
        if tstr <> "":
           tstr = tstr + vbtab

        tstr = tstr + '"' + rs.Fields(x).Value + '"'

      txtstream.Writeline(tstr)
      tstr = ""
      rs.MoveNext
```

TAB DELIMITED VERTICAL

```
    for x = 0 in rs.fields.count:
      tstr = rs.Fields(x).Name
      rs.MoveFirst()
```

```
        while rs.eof = false:
            if tstr <> "":
                tstr = tstr + vbtab

            tstr = tstr + '"' + rs.Fields(x).Value + '"'
            rs.MoveNext

        txtstream.Writeline(tstr)
        tstr = ""


        txtstream.Close
```

```
    ws = win32com.client.Dispatch("WScript.Shell")
    fso = win32com.client.Dispatch("Scripting.FileSystemObject")
    txtstream = fso.OpenTextFile(ws.CurrentDirectory + "\Products.txt", 2, True, -
2)
    tstr= ""
Horizontal
    for x = 0 in rs.fields.count:
        if tstr <> "":
            tstr = tstr + "~"

        tstr = tstr + rs.Fields(x).Name

    txtstream.Writeline(tstr)
    tstr = ""
    rs.MoveFirst()
    while rs.eof = false:
        for x = 0 in rs.fields.count:
            if tstr <> "":
                tstr = tstr + "~"

            tstr = tstr + '"' + rs.Fields(x).Value + '"'
```

```
        txtstream.Writeline(tstr)
        tstr = ""
        rs.MoveNext
```

TILDE DELIMITED VERTICAL

```
   for x = 0 in rs.fields.count:
       tstr = rs.Fields(x).Name
       rs.MoveFirst()
       while rs.eof = false:
           if tstr <> "":
               tstr = tstr + "~"

           tstr = tstr + '"' + rs.Fields(x).Value + '"'
           rs.MoveNext

       txtstream.Writeline(tstr)
       tstr = ""

       txtstream.Close
```

XML FILES

I

In this section of the book, we're going to be Coding for the creation of Attribute XML Element XML, Element XML for XSL and Schema XML

```
import win32com.client
import string
```

ATTRIBUTE XML USING A TEXT FILE

```
ws = Win32com.client.Dispatch("WScript.Shell")
fso = Win32com.client.Dispatch("Scripting.FileSystemObject")
txtstream = fso.OpenTextFile("C:\Products.xml", 2, True, -2)
txtstream.WriteLine("<?xml version='1.0' encoding='iso-8859-1'?>")
txtstream.WriteLine("<data>")
rs.MoveFirst()
While rs.EOF = false:
    txtstream.WriteLine("<Products>")
    For x in range(rs.Fields.Count):
        txtstream.WriteLine("<property name = """ + rs.Fields[x].Name + """
value=""" + rs.Fields[x].value + """/>")

    txtstream.WriteLine("</Products>")
  rs.MoveNext()
```

```
txtstream.WriteLine("</data>")
txtstream.Close
```

ATTRIBUTE XML USING THE DOM

```
xmldoc  = win32com.client.Dispatch("MSXML2.DOMDocument")
pi      =       xmldoc.CreateProcessingInstruction("xml",      "version='1.0'
encoding='ISO-8859-1'")
oRoot = xmldoc.CreateElement("data")
xmldoc.AppendChild(pi)
while rs.EOF  == False:
  oNode = xmldoc.CreateNode(1, "Win32_Process", "")
  for x in range(rs.Fields.Count):
    oNode1 = xmldoc.CreateNode(1, "Property", "")
    oAtt = xmldoc.CreateAttribute("NAME")
    oAtt.Value = rs.Fields[x].Name
    oNode1.Attributes.SetNamedItem(oAtt)
    oAtt = xmldoc.CreateAttribute("DATATYPE")
    oAtt.Value = str(rs.Fields[x].Type.Name))
    oNode1.Attributes.SetNamedItem(oAtt)
    oAtt = xmldoc.CreateAttribute("SIZE")
    oAtt.Value = str(rs.Fields[x].Value.)
    oNode1.Attributes.SetNamedItem(oAtt)
    oAtt = xmldoc.CreateAttribute("Value")
    oAtt.Value = GetValue(prop, obj)
    oNode1.Attributes.SetNamedItem(oAtt)
    oNode.AppendChild(oNode1)

  oRoot.AppendChild(oNode)

xmldoc.AppendChild(oRoot)
ws = win32com.client.Dispatch("WScript.Shell")
xmldoc.Save(ws.CurrentDirectory + "\\Products.xml")
```

ELEMENT XML USING A TEXT FILE

```
ws = win32com.client.Dispatch("WScript.Shell")
fso = win32com.client.Dispatch("Scripting.FileSystemObject")
txtstream = fso.OpenTextFile(ws.CurrentDirectory + "\Products.txt", 2, True, -
2)
txtstream.WriteLine("<?xml version='1.0' encoding='iso-8859-1'?>")
txtstream.WriteLine("<data>")
rs.MoveFirst
while rs.eof = false:
   txtstream.WriteLine("<Products>")
   for x = 0 in rs.fields.count:
      txtstream.WriteLine("<" + rs.Fields(x).Name + ">" + rs.Fields(x).Value +
"</" + rs.Fields(x).Name + ">")

   txtstream.WriteLine("</Products>")
   rs.MoveNext()

txtstream.WriteLine("</data>")
txtstream.close()
```

ELEMENT XML USING THE DOM

```
xmldoc  = win32com.client.Dispatch("MSXML2.DOMDocument")
pi      =      xmldoc.CreateProcessingInstruction("xml",      "version='1.0'
encoding='ISO-8859-1'")
oRoot = xmldoc.CreateElement("data")
xmldoc.AppendChild(pi)
while rs.EOF  == False:
   oNode = xmldoc.CreateNode(1, "Win32_Process", "")
   for x in range(rs.Fields.Count):
      oNode1 = xmldoc.CreateNode(1, rs.Fields[x],Name, "")
      oNode1.Text = str(rs.Fields[x].Value)
      oNode.AppendChild(oNode1)
```

```
    oRoot.AppendChild(oNode)

    xmldoc.AppendChild(oRoot)
    ws = win32com.client.Dispatch("WScript.Shell")
    xmldoc.Save(ws.CurrentDirectory + "\\Products.xml")
```

ELEMENT XML FOR XSL USING A TEXT FILE

```
    ws = win32com.client.Dispatch("WScript.Shell")
    fso = win32com.client.Dispatch("Scripting.FileSystemObject")
    txtstream = fso.OpenTextFile(ws.CurrentDirectory + "\Products.txt", 2, True, -
2)
    txtstream.WriteLine("<?xml version='1.0' encoding='iso-8859-1'?>")
    txtstream.WriteLine("<?xml-stylesheet        type='Text/xsl'        href='"        +
ws.CurrentDirectory + "\Products.xsl"?>
    rs.MoveFirst
    while rs.eof = false:
       txtstream.WriteLine("<Products>")
       for x = 0 in rs.fields.count:
          txtstream.WriteLine("<" + rs.Fields(x).Name + ">" + rs.Fields(x).Value +
"</" + rs.Fields(x).Name + ">")

       txtstream.WriteLine("</Products>")
       rs.MoveNext()

    txtstream.WriteLine("</data>")
    txtstream.close()
```

ELEMENT XML FOR XSL USING THE DOM

```
xmldoc  = win32com.client.Dispatch("MSXML2.DOMDocument")
  pi = xmldoc.CreateProcessingInstruction("xml", "version='1.0' encoding='ISO-
  8859-1'")
```

```
    pii  =  xmldoc.CreateProcessingInstruction("xml-stylesheet",  "type='text/xsl'
href='Process.xsl'")
    oRoot = xmldoc.CreateElement("data")
    xmldoc.AppendChild(pi)
    xmldoc.AppendChild(pii)

        while rs.EOF  == False:
          oNode = xmldoc.CreateNode(1, "Win32_Process", "")
          for x in range(rs.Fields.Count):
            oNode1 = xmldoc.CreateNode(1, rs.Fields[x],Name, "")
            oNode1.Text = str(rs.Fields[x].Value)
            oNode.AppendChild(oNode1)

          oRoot.AppendChild(oNode)

        xmldoc.AppendChild(oRoot)
        ws = win32com.client.Dispatch("WScript.Shell")
        xmldoc.Save(ws.CurrentDirectory + "\\Products.xml")
```

Schema XML Using A Text File

```
      ws = win32com.client.Dispatch("WScript.Shell")
      fso = win32com.client.Dispatch("Scripting.FileSystemObject")
      txtstream = fso.OpenTextFile(ws.CurrentDirectory + "\Products.txt", 2, True, -
2)
      txtstream.WriteLine("<?xml version='1.0' encoding='iso-8859-1'?>")
      txtstream.WriteLine("<data>")
      rs.MoveFirst
      while rs.eof = false:
        txtstream.WriteLine("<Products>")
        for x = 0 in rs.fields.count:
          txtstream.WriteLine("<" + rs.Fields(x).Name + ">" + rs.Fields(x).Value +
"</" + rs.Fields(x).Name + ">")

        txtstream.WriteLine("</Products>")
        rs.MoveNext()

      txtstream.WriteLine("</data>")
      txtstream.close()
```

```
rs1 = win32com.client.Dispatch("ADODB.Recordset")
rs1.ActiveConnection              =              "Provider=MSDAOSP;              Data
Source=msxml2.DSOControl"
rs1.Open(ws.CurrentDirectory + "\Products.xml")

If (fso.FileExists(ws.CurrentDirectory + "\Products_Schema.xml") = True)
Then
    fso.DeleteFile(ws.CurrentDirectory + "\Products_Schema.xml")


rs.Save(ws.CurrentDirectory + "\Products_Schema.xml", 1)
```

Schema XML Using the DOM

```
xmldoc = win32com.client.Dispatch("MSXML2.DOMDocument")
pi     =     xmldoc.CreateProcessingInstruction("xml",     "version='1.0'
encoding='ISO-8859-1'")
oRoot = xmldoc.CreateElement("data")
xmldoc.AppendChild(pi)
while rs.EOF == False:
    oNode = xmldoc.CreateNode(1, "Win32_Process", "")
    for x in range(rs.Fields.Count):
        oNode1 = xmldoc.CreateNode(1, rs.Fields[x],Name, "")
        oNode1.Text = str(rs.Fields[x].Value)
        oNode.AppendChild(oNode1)

    oRoot.AppendChild(oNode)

xmldoc.AppendChild(oRoot)
ws = win32com.client.Dispatch("WScript.Shell")
xmldoc.Save(ws.CurrentDirectory + "\\Products.xml")


rs1 = win32com.client.Dispatch("ADODB.Recordset")
rs1.ActiveConnection              =              "Provider=MSDAOSP;              Data
Source=msxml2.DSOControl"
rs1.Open(ws.CurrentDirectory + "\Products.xml")
```

```
        If  (fso.FileExists(ws.CurrentDirectory  +  "\Products_Schema.xml")  =  True)
Then
            fso.DeleteFile(ws.CurrentDirectory + "\Products_Schema.xml")


        rs.Save(ws.CurrentDirectory + "\Products_Schema.xml", 1)
```

EXCEL CODING EXAMPLES

B

ELOW ARE SOME EXAMPLES OF ADO DRIVING EXCEL VISUAL RENDERINGS.

EXCEL CODE IN HORIZONTAL FORMAT USING A CSV FILE

```
ws = win32com.client.Dispatch("WScript.Shell")
fso = win32com.client.Dispatch("Scripting.FileSystemObject")
txtstream = fso.OpenTextFile(ws.CurrentDirectory + "\Products.csv", 2, True,
-2)
tstr= ""


for x = 0 in rs.fields.count:
   if tstr <> "":
      tstr = tstr + ","

   tstr = tstr + rs.Fields(x).Name

txtstream.Writeline(tstr)
tstr = ""
rs.MoveFirst()
while rs.eof = false:
   for x = 0 in rs.fields.count:
      if tstr <> "":
         tstr = tstr + ","
```

```
    tstr = tstr + '"' + rs.Fields(x).Value + '"'

  txtstream.Writeline(tstr)
  tstr = ""
  rs.MoveNext
```

EXCEL CODE IN VERTICAL FORMAT USING A CSV FILE

```
ws = win32com.client.Dispatch("WScript.Shell")
fso = win32com.client.Dispatch("Scripting.FileSystemObject")
txtstream = fso.OpenTextFile(ws.CurrentDirectory + "\Products.csv", 2, True,
-2)
  tstr= ""


for x = 0 in rs.fields.count:
  tstr = rs.Fields(x).Name
  rs.MoveFirst()
  while rs.eof = false:
    if tstr <> "":
      tstr = tstr + ","

    tstr = tstr + '"' + rs.Fields(x).Value + '"'
    rs.MoveNext

  txtstream.Writeline(tstr)
  tstr = ""

txtstream.Close

ws.Run(ws.CurrentDirectory + "\Products.csv")
```

EXCEL USING HORIZONTAL FORMAT AUTOMATION CODE

```
oExcel = win32com.client.Dispatch("Excel.Application")
oExcel.Visible = true
wb = oExcel.Workbooks.Add()
```

```
ws = wb.WorkSheets(1)
ws.Name = "Products"
x=1
y=2
for z in 1..rs.fields.count-1 do
   ws.Cells.Item(1, x) = rs.Fields(z).Name
   x=x+1

x=1
rs.MoveFirst()
Do While rs.EOF = False
   for z in 1..rs.fields.count-1 do
      ws.Cells.Item(y, x) = rs.Fields(z).Value
      x=x+1

   x=1
   y=y+1
   rs.MoveNext


ws.Columns.HorizontalAlignment = -4131
iret = ws.Columns.AutoFit()
```

EXCEL USING VERTICAL FORMAT AUTOMATION CODE

```
oExcel = win32com.client.Dispatch("Excel.Application")
oExcel.Visible = true
wb = oExcel.Workbooks.Add()
ws = wb.WorkSheets(1)
ws.Name = "Products"
x=1
y=2
for z in 1..rs.fields.count-1 do
   ws.Cells.Item(x, 1) = rs.Fields(z).Name
   x=x+1

x=1
rs.MoveFirst()
```

```
Do While rs.EOF = False
    for z in 1..rs.fields.count-1 do
        ws.Cells.Item(x, y) = rs.Fields(z).Value
        x=x+1

    x=1
    y=y+1
    rs.MoveNext


ws.Columns.HorizontalAlignment = -4131
iret = ws.Columns.AutoFit()
```

EXCEL SPREADSHEET EXAMPLE

```
ws = win32com.client.Dispatch("WScript.Shell")
fso = win32com.client.Dispatch("Scripting.FileSystemObject")
txtstream = fso.OpenTextFile(ws.CurrentDirectory + "\\ProcessExcel.xml", 2,
True, -2)
txtstream.WriteLine("<?xml version='1.0'?>")
txtstream.WriteLine("<?mso-application progid='Excel.Sheet'?>")
txtstream.WriteLine("<Workbook                xmlns='urn:schemas-microsoft-
com:office:spreadsheet'        xmlns:o='urn:schemas-microsoft-com:office:office'
xmlns:x='urn:schemas-microsoft-com:office:excel'        xmlns:ss='urn:schemas-
microsoft-com:office:spreadsheet'      xmlns:html='http://www.w3.org/TR/REC-
html40'>")
txtstream.WriteLine("  <DocumentProperties   xmlns='urn:schemas-microsoft-
com:office:office'>")
txtstream.WriteLine("        <Author>Windows User</Author>")
txtstream.WriteLine("        <LastAuthor>Windows User</LastAuthor>")
txtstream.WriteLine("        <Created>2007-11-27T19:36:16Z</Created>")
txtstream.WriteLine("        <Version>12.00</Version>")
txtstream.WriteLine("  </DocumentProperties>")
txtstream.WriteLine("  <ExcelWorkbook            xmlns='urn:schemas-microsoft-
com:office:excel'>")
txtstream.WriteLine("        <WindowHeight>11835</WindowHeight>")
```

```
txtstream.WriteLine("          <WindowWidth>18960</WindowWidth>")
txtstream.WriteLine("          <WindowTopX>120</WindowTopX>")
txtstream.WriteLine("          <WindowTopY>135</WindowTopY>")
txtstream.WriteLine("          <ProtectStructure>False</ProtectStructure>")
txtstream.WriteLine("          <ProtectWindows>False</ProtectWindows>")
txtstream.WriteLine(" </ExcelWorkbook>")
txtstream.WriteLine(" <Styles>")
txtstream.WriteLine("          <Style ss:ID='Default' ss:Name='Normal'>")
txtstream.WriteLine("              <Alignment ss:Vertical='Bottom'/>")
txtstream.WriteLine("              <Borders/>")
txtstream.WriteLine("              <Font          ss:FontName='Calibri'
x:Family='Swiss' ss:Size='11' ss:Color='#000000'/>")
txtstream.WriteLine("              <Interior/>")
txtstream.WriteLine("              <NumberFormat/>")
txtstream.WriteLine("              <Protection/>")
txtstream.WriteLine("          </Style>")
txtstream.WriteLine("          <Style ss:ID='s62'>")
txtstream.WriteLine("              <Borders/>")
txtstream.WriteLine("              <Font          ss:FontName='Calibri'
x:Family='Swiss' ss:Size='11' ss:Color='#000000' ss:Bold='1'/>")
txtstream.WriteLine("          </Style>")
txtstream.WriteLine("          <Style ss:ID='s63'>")
txtstream.WriteLine("              <Alignment          ss:Horizontal='Left'
ss:Vertical='Bottom' ss:Indent='2'/>")
txtstream.WriteLine("              <Font          ss:FontName='Verdana'
x:Family='Swiss' ss:Size='7.7' ss:Color='#000000'/>")
txtstream.WriteLine("          </Style>")
txtstream.WriteLine(" </Styles>")

txtstream.WriteLine("<Worksheet ss:Name='Process'>")
txtstream.WriteLine("          <Table     x:FullColumns='1'     x:FullRows='1'
ss:DefaultRowHeight='24.9375'>")
txtstream.WriteLine("          <Column  ss:AutoFitWidth='1'  ss:Width='82.5'
ss:Span='5'/>")
txtstream.WriteLine("  <Row ss:AutoFitHeight='0'>")
for x in range(rs.Fields.Count):
    txtstream.WriteLine("              <Cell   ss:StyleID='s62'><Data
ss:Type='String'>" + rs.Fields[x].Name + "</Data></Cell>")

    txtstream.WriteLine("     </Row>")
```

```
    while rs.EOF == False:
      txtstream.WriteLine("      <Row ss:AutoFitHeight='0' ss:Height='13.5'>")
      for x in range(rs.Fields.Count):
        txtstream.WriteLine("            <Cell><Data ss:Type='String'><![CDATA[" +
str(rs.Fields[x].Value)) + "]]></Data></Cell>")

      txtstream.WriteLine("      </Row>")


    txtstream.WriteLine("  </Table>")
    txtstream.WriteLine("  <WorksheetOptions       xmlns='urn:schemas-microsoft-
com:office:excel'>")
    txtstream.WriteLine("            <PageSetup>")
    txtstream.WriteLine("                <Header x:Margin='0.3'/>")
    txtstream.WriteLine("                <Footer x:Margin='0.3'/>")
    txtstream.WriteLine("                <PageMargins        x:Bottom='0.75'
x:Left='0.7' x:Right='0.7' x:Top='0.75'/>")
    txtstream.WriteLine("            </PageSetup>")
    txtstream.WriteLine("            <Unsynced/>")
    txtstream.WriteLine("        <Print>")
    txtstream.WriteLine("                <FitHeight>0</FitHeight>")
    txtstream.WriteLine("                <ValidPrinterInfo/>")
    txtstream.WriteLine("
      <HorizontalResolution>600</HorizontalResolution>")
    txtstream.WriteLine("
      <VerticalResolution>600</VerticalResolution>")
    txtstream.WriteLine("            </Print>")
    txtstream.WriteLine("        <Selected/>")
    txtstream.WriteLine("        <Panes>")
    txtstream.WriteLine("            <Pane>")
    txtstream.WriteLine("                    <Number>3</Number>")
    txtstream.WriteLine("                    <ActiveRow>9</ActiveRow>")
    txtstream.WriteLine("                    <ActiveCol>7</ActiveCol>")
    txtstream.WriteLine("            </Pane>")
    txtstream.WriteLine("        </Panes>")
    txtstream.WriteLine("        <ProtectObjects>False</ProtectObjects>")
    txtstream.WriteLine("        <ProtectScenarios>False</ProtectScenarios>")
    txtstream.WriteLine("  </WorksheetOptions>")
    txtstream.WriteLine("</Worksheet>")
```

```
txtstream.WriteLine("</Workbook>")
txtstream.Close()
ws.Run(ws.CurrentDirectory + "\\Products.xml")
```

CREATING XSL FILES

B

ELOW are examples of creating XSL files.

```
ws = win32com.client.Dispatch("WScript.Shell")
fso = win32com.client.Dispatch("Scripting.FileSystemObject")
txtstream = fso.OpenTextFile(ws.CurrentDirectory + "\Products.xsl", 2, true, -
2)
txtstream.WriteLine("<?xml version='1.0' encoding='UTF-8'?>")
txtstream.WriteLine("<xsl:stylesheet                    version='1.0'
xmlns:xsl='http://www.w3.org/1999/XSL/Transform'>")
txtstream.WriteLine("<xsl:template match=""/"">")
txtstream.WriteLine("<html>")
txtstream.WriteLine("<head>")
txtstream.WriteLine("<title>Products</title>")
txtstream.WriteLine("</head>")
#Add Stylesheet Here
txtstream.WriteLine("<body>")
rs.MoveFirst()
```

```
txtstream.WriteLine("<table border='0' Cellpadding='2' cellspacing='2>")
```

```vb
txtstream.WriteLine("<tr>")
for x = 0 to rs.Fields.count-1
    txtstream.WriteLine("<th align='left' nowrap='true'>" + rs.Fields(x).Name
+ "</th>")

txtstream.WriteLine("</tr>")
txtstream.WriteLine("<tr>")
for x = 0 to rs.Fields.count-1
```

NONE
```vb
    txtstream.WriteLine("<td><xsl:value-of      select=""data/Products/" +
rs.Fields(x).Name + """/></td>")
```

BUTTON
```vb
    txtstream.WriteLine("<td          align='left'     nowrap='true'><button
style='width:100%;'><xsl:value-of select=""data/Products/" + rs.Fields(x).Name +
"""/></button></td>")
```

COMBOBOX
```vb
    txtstream.WriteLine("<td                              align='left'
nowrap='true'><select><option><xsl:attribute         name='value'><xsl:value-of
select=""data/Products/" + rs.Fields(x).Name + """/></xsl:attribute><xsl:value-of
select=""data/Products/" + rs.Fields(x).Name + """/></option></select></td>")
```

DIV
```vb
    txtstream.WriteLine("<td  align='left' nowrap='true'><div><xsl:value-of
select=""data/Products/" + rs.Fields(x).Name + """/></div></td>")
```

LINK
```vb
    txtstream.WriteLine("<td      align='left' nowrap='true'><a  href='" +
rs.Fields(x).Value + "'><xsl:value-of select=""data/Products/" + rs.Fields(x).Name
+ """/></a></td>")
```

LISTBOX
```vb
    txtstream.WriteLine("<td          align='left'     nowrap='true'><select
multiple><option><xsl:attribute                            name='value'><xsl:value-of
```

```
select="""data/Products/" + rs.Fields(x).Name  + """"/></xsl:attribute><xsl:value-of
select="""data/Products/" + rs.Fields(x).Name  + """"/></option></select></td>")
```

```
        txtstream.WriteLine("<td   align='left'  nowrap='true'><span><xsl:value-
of select="""data/Products/" + rs.Fields(x).Name  + """"/></span></td>")
```

```
        txtstream.WriteLine("<td                                        align='left'
nowrap='true'><textarea><xsl:value-of        select="""data/Products/"        +
rs.Fields(x).Name  + """"/></textarea></td>")
```

```
        txtstream.WriteLine("<td         align='left'      nowrap='true'><input
type='text'><xsl:attribute name=""value""><xsl:value-of select="""data/Products/"
+ rs.Fields(x).Name  + """"/></xsl:attribute></input></td>")
```

```
    txtstream.WriteLine("</tr>")
```

MULTI LINE HORIZONTAL REPORTS

```
    txtstream.WriteLine("<table border='0' Cellpadding='2' cellspacing='2>")


    txtstream.WriteLine("<tr>")
    for x = 0 to rs.Fields.count-1
       txtstream.WriteLine("<th>" + rs.Fields(x).Name + "</th>")

    txtstream.WriteLine("</tr>")
    txtstream.WriteLine("<xsl:for-each select="""data/Products""">")
    txtstream.WriteLine("<tr>")
    for x = 0 to rs.Fields.count-1
       txtstream.WriteLine("<td><xsl:value-of select="" " + rs.Fields(x).Name + "
""/></td>")
```

```
txtstream.WriteLine("<td><xsl:value-of select="""" + rs.Fields(x).Name +
"""/></td>")
```

BUTTON

```
txtstream.WriteLine("<td          align='left'      nowrap='true'><button
style='width:100%;'><xsl:value-of   select=""""   +   rs.Fields(x).Name      +
"""/></button></td>")
```
COMBOBOX

```
txtstream.WriteLine("<td                                          align='left'
nowrap='true'><select><option><xsl:attribute         name='value'><xsl:value-of
select=""""    +    rs.Fields(x).Name        +      """/></xsl:attribute><xsl:value-of
select=""data/Products/" + rs.Fields(x).Name  + """/></option></select></td>")
```

DIV

```
txtstream.WriteLine("<td   align='left' nowrap='true'><div><xsl:value-of
select=""data/Products/" + rs.Fields(x).Name  + """/></div></td>")
```

LINK

```
txtstream.WriteLine("<td      align='left' nowrap='true'><a href='"  +
rs.Fields(x).Value + "'><xsl:value-of select=""data/Products/" + rs.Fields(x).Name
+ """/></a></td>")
```

LISTBOX

```
txtstream.WriteLine("<td               align='left'       nowrap='true'><select
multiple><option><xsl:attribute                        name='value'><xsl:value-of
select=""data/Products/" + rs.Fields(x).Name  + """/></xsl:attribute><xsl:value-of
select=""data/Products/" + rs.Fields(x).Name  + """/></option></select></td>")
```

SPAN

```
txtstream.WriteLine("<td   align='left' nowrap='true'><span><xsl:value-
of select=""data/Products/" + rs.Fields(x).Name  + """/></span></td>")
```

TEXTAREA

```
        txtstream.WriteLine("<td                                    align='left'
nowrap='true'><textarea><xsl:value-of          select=""data/Products/"         +
rs.Fields(x).Name  + """/></textarea></td>")
```

TEXTBOX

```
        txtstream.WriteLine("<td          align='left'       nowrap='true'><input
type='text'><xsl:attribute name=""value""><xsl:value-of select=""data/Products/"
+ rs.Fields(x).Name  + """/></xsl:attribute></input></td>")
```

```
    txtstream.WriteLine("</tr>")
    txtstream.WriteLine("</xsl:for-each>")
```

SINGLE LINE VERTICAL REPORTS

```
    for x = 0 to rs.Fields.count-1
        txtstream.WriteLine("<tr><th>" + rs.Fields(x).Name + "</th>")
```

NONE

```
        txtstream.WriteLine("<td><xsl:value-of       select=""data/Products/"      +
rs.Fields(x).Name  + """/></td></tr>")
```

BUTTON

```
        txtstream.WriteLine("<td            align='left'      nowrap='true'><button
style='width:100%;'><xsl:value-of select=""data/Products/" + rs.Fields(x).Name  +
"""/></button></td></tr>")
```

COMBOBOX

```
        txtstream.WriteLine("<td                                    align='left'
nowrap='true'><select><option><xsl:attribute          name='value'><xsl:value-of
select=""data/Products/" + rs.Fields(x).Name  + """/></xsl:attribute><xsl:value-of
select=""data/Products/"         +         rs.Fields(x).Name                    +
"""/></option></select></td></tr>")
```

DIV

```
txtstream.WriteLine("<td  align='left' nowrap='true'><div><xsl:value-of
select=""data/Products/" + rs.Fields(x).Name + """/></div></td></tr>")
```

LINK

```
txtstream.WriteLine("<td    align='left'  nowrap='true'><a  href='" +
rs.Fields(x).Value + "'><xsl:value-of select=""data/Products/" + rs.Fields(x).Name
+ """/></a></td></tr>")
```

LISTBOX

```
txtstream.WriteLine("<td                align='left'      nowrap='true'><select
multiple><option><xsl:attribute                    name='value'><xsl:value-of
select=""data/Products/" + rs.Fields(x).Name  + """/></xsl:attribute><xsl:value-of
select=""data/Products/"          +          rs.Fields(x).Name                +
"""/></option></select></td></tr>")
```
SPAN

```
txtstream.WriteLine("<td  align='left' nowrap='true'><span><xsl:value-
of select=""data/Products/" + rs.Fields(x).Name  + """/></span></td></tr>")
```

TEXTAREA

```
txtstream.WriteLine("<td                                      align='left'
nowrap='true'><textarea><xsl:value-of          select=""data/Products/"          +
rs.Fields(x).Name + """/></textarea></td></tr>")
```

TEXTBOX

```
txtstream.WriteLine("<td          align='left'      nowrap='true'><input
type='text'><xsl:attribute name=""value""><xsl:value-of select=""data/Products/"
+ rs.Fields(x).Name + """/></xsl:attribute></input></td></tr>")
```

MULTI LINE VERTICAL REPORTS

```
txtstream.WriteLine("<table border='0' Cellpadding='2' cellspacing='2>")
```

```
for x = 0 to rs.Fields.count-1
```

txtstream.WriteLine("<tr><th   align='left'   nowrap='true'>"   + rs.Fields(x).Name + "</th>")

NONE

txtstream.WriteLine("<xsl:for-each   select=""data/Products"">"<td align='left'   nowrap='true'><xsl:value-of   select="""   +   rs.Fields(x).Name   + """"/></td></xsl:for-each></tr>")

BUTTON

txtstream.WriteLine("<xsl:for-each   select=""data/Products"">"<td align='left' nowrap='true'><button style='width:100%;'><xsl:value-of select=""" + rs.Fields(x).Name + """"/></button></td></xsl:for-each></tr>")

COMBOBOX

txtstream.WriteLine("<xsl:for-each   select=""data/Products"">"<td align='left'   nowrap='true'><select><option><xsl:attribute name='value'><xsl:value-of   select="""   +   rs.Fields(x).Name   + """"/></xsl:attribute><xsl:value-of select=""data/Products/" + rs.Fields(x).Name   + """"/></option></select></td></xsl:for-each></tr>")

DIV

txtstream.WriteLine("<xsl:for-each   select=""data/Products"">"<td align='left'   nowrap='true'> <xsl:value-of   select=""data/Products/"   + rs.Fields(x).Name + """"/> </td></xsl:for-each></tr>")

LINK

txtstream.WriteLine("<xsl:for-each   select=""data/Products"">"<td align='left' nowrap='true'><a href='" + rs.Fields(x).Value + "'><xsl:value-of select=""data/Products/"   +   rs.Fields(x).Name   +   """"/></a></td></xsl:for-each></tr>")

LISTBOX

txtstream.WriteLine("<xsl:for-each   select=""data/Products"">"<td align='left'   nowrap='true'><select   multiple><option><xsl:attribute name='value'><xsl:value-of   select=""data/Products/"   +   rs.Fields(x).Name   +

```
"""/></xsl:attribute><xsl:value-of select=""data/Products/" + rs.Fields(x).Name +
"""/></option></select></td></xsl:for-each></tr>")
```

SPAN

```
        txtstream.WriteLine("<xsl:for-each        select=""data/Products"">><td
align='left'   nowrap='true'><span><xsl:value-of   select=""data/Products/"   +
rs.Fields(x).Name + """/></span></td></xsl:for-each></tr>")
```

TEXTAREA

```
        txtstream.WriteLine("<xsl:for-each        select=""data/Products"">><td
align='left'  nowrap='true'><textarea><xsl:value-of  select=""data/Products/"  +
rs.Fields(x).Name + """/></textarea></td></xsl:for-each></tr>")
```

TEXTBOX

```
        txtstream.WriteLine("<xsl:for-each        select=""data/Products"">><td
align='left'           nowrap='true'><input           type='text'><xsl:attribute
name=""value""><xsl:value-of select=""data/Products/" + rs.Fields(x).Name +
"""/></xsl:attribute></input></td></xsl:for-each></tr>")
```

SINGLE LINE HORIZONTAL TABLES

```
   txtstream.WriteLine("<table       style='border:Double;border-width:1px;border-
color:navy;' rules=all frames=both cellpadding=2 cellspacing=2 Width=0>")


    txtstream.WriteLine("<tr>")
    for x = 0 to rs.Fields.count-1
       txtstream.WriteLine("<th align='left' nowrap='true'>" + rs.Fields(x).Name
+ "</th>")

    txtstream.WriteLine("</tr>")
    txtstream.WriteLine("<tr>")
    for x = 0 to rs.Fields.count-1
```

NONE

```
        txtstream.WriteLine("<td><xsl:value-of        select=""data/Products/"        +
rs.Fields(x).Name  + """/></td>")
```

BUTTON

```
        txtstream.WriteLine("<td        align='left'        nowrap='true'><button
style='width:100%;'><xsl:value-of select=""data/Products/" + rs.Fields(x).Name  +
"""/></button></td>")
```

COMBOBOX

```
        txtstream.WriteLine("<td                                        align='left'
nowrap='true'><select><option><xsl:attribute        name='value'><xsl:value-of
select=""data/Products/" + rs.Fields(x).Name  + """/></xsl:attribute><xsl:value-of
select=""data/Products/" + rs.Fields(x).Name  + """/></option></select></td>")
```

DIV

```
        txtstream.WriteLine("<td  align='left' nowrap='true'><div><xsl:value-of
select=""data/Products/" + rs.Fields(x).Name  + """/></div></td>")
```

LINK

```
        txtstream.WriteLine("<td        align='left'  nowrap='true'><a  href='"   +
rs.Fields(x).Value + "'><xsl:value-of select=""data/Products/"  + rs.Fields(x).Name
+ """/></a></td>")
```

LISTBOX

```
        txtstream.WriteLine("<td        align='left'        nowrap='true'><select
multiple><option><xsl:attribute                name='value'><xsl:value-of
select=""data/Products/" + rs.Fields(x).Name  + """/></xsl:attribute><xsl:value-of
select=""data/Products/" + rs.Fields(x).Name  + """/></option></select></td>")
```

SPAN

```
        txtstream.WriteLine("<td  align='left' nowrap='true'><span><xsl:value-
of select=""data/Products/" + rs.Fields(x).Name  + """/></span></td>")
```

TEXTAREA

```
txtstream.WriteLine("<td                                         align='left'
nowrap='true'><textarea><xsl:value-of         select=""data/Products/"         +
rs.Fields(x).Name  + """/></textarea></td>")
```

```
        txtstream.WriteLine("<td         align='left'     nowrap='true'><input
type='text'><xsl:attribute name=""value""><xsl:value-of select=""data/Products/"
+ rs.Fields(x).Name  + """/></xsl:attribute></input></td>")
```

```
    txtstream.WriteLine("</tr>")
```

MULTI LINE HORIZONTAL TABLES

```
txtstream.WriteLine("<table         style='border:Double;border-width:1px;border-
color:navy;' rules=all frames=both cellpadding=2 cellspacing=2 Width=0>")
```

```
    txtstream.WriteLine("<tr>")
    for x = 0 to rs.Fields.count-1
       txtstream.WriteLine("<th>" + rs.Fields(x).Name + "</th>")

    txtstream.WriteLine("</tr>")
    txtstream.WriteLine("<xsl:for-each select=""data/Products"">")
    txtstream.WriteLine("<tr>")
    for x = 0 to rs.Fields.count-1
       txtstream.WriteLine("<td><xsl:value-of select="" " + rs.Fields(x).Name + "
""/></td>")
```

```
        txtstream.WriteLine("<td><xsl:value-of select=""" + rs.Fields(x).Name   +
"""/></td>")
```

```vb
        txtstream.WriteLine("<td            align='left'      nowrap='true'><button
style='width:100%;'><xsl:value-of      select="""      +      rs.Fields(x).Name      +
"""/></button></td>")
```

COMBOBOX

```vb
        txtstream.WriteLine("<td                                        align='left'
nowrap='true'><select><option><xsl:attribute          name='value'><xsl:value-of
select="""     +     rs.Fields(x).Name     +      """/></xsl:attribute><xsl:value-of
select=""data/Products/" + rs.Fields(x).Name + """/></option></select></td>")
```

DIV

```vb
        txtstream.WriteLine("<td   align='left' nowrap='true'><div><xsl:value-of
select=""data/Products/" + rs.Fields(x).Name  + """/></div></td>")
```

LINK

```vb
        txtstream.WriteLine("<td      align='left'  nowrap='true'><a  href='"  +
rs.Fields(x).Value + "'><xsl:value-of select=""data/Products/"  + rs.Fields(x).Name
+ """/></a></td>")
```

LISTBOX

```vb
        txtstream.WriteLine("<td            align='left'      nowrap='true'><select
multiple><option><xsl:attribute                name='value'><xsl:value-of
select=""data/Products/" + rs.Fields(x).Name  + """/></xsl:attribute><xsl:value-of
select=""data/Products/" + rs.Fields(x).Name  + """/></option></select></td>")
```

SPAN

```vb
        txtstream.WriteLine("<td   align='left' nowrap='true'><span><xsl:value-
of select=""data/Products/" + rs.Fields(x).Name  + """/></span></td>")
```

TEXTAREA

```vb
        txtstream.WriteLine("<td                                        align='left'
nowrap='true'><textarea><xsl:value-of        select=""data/Products/"        +
rs.Fields(x).Name  + """/></textarea></td>")
```

TEXTBOX

```
txtstream.WriteLine("<td                align='left'      nowrap='true'><input
type='text'><xsl:attribute name=""value""><xsl:value-of select=""data/Products/"
+ rs.Fields(x).Name  + """/></xsl:attribute></input></td>")

txtstream.WriteLine("</tr>")
txtstream.WriteLine("</xsl:for-each>")
```

SINGLE LINE VERTICAL TABLES

```
for x = 0 to rs.Fields.count-1
    txtstream.WriteLine("<tr><th>" + rs.Fields(x).Name + "</th>")
```

NONE

```
txtstream.WriteLine("<td><xsl:value-of       select=""data/Products/"       +
rs.Fields(x).Name  + """/></td></tr>")
```

BUTTON

```
txtstream.WriteLine("<td            align='left'     nowrap='true'><button
style='width:100%;'><xsl:value-of select=""data/Products/" + rs.Fields(x).Name  +
"""/></button></td></tr>")
```

COMBOBOX

```
txtstream.WriteLine("<td                                       align='left'
nowrap='true'><select><option><xsl:attribute       name='value'><xsl:value-of
select=""data/Products/" + rs.Fields(x).Name  + """/></xsl:attribute><xsl:value-of
select=""data/Products/"       +       rs.Fields(x).Name                 +
"""/></option></select></td></tr>")
```

DIV

```
txtstream.WriteLine("<td   align='left' nowrap='true'><div><xsl:value-of
select=""data/Products/" + rs.Fields(x).Name  + """/></div></td></tr>")
```

LINK

```
        txtstream.WriteLine("<td      align='left'  nowrap='true'><a  href='"  +
rs.Fields(x).Value + "'><xsl:value-of select=""data/Products/" + rs.Fields(x).Name
+ """/></a></td></tr>")
```

LISTBOX

```
        txtstream.WriteLine("<td          align='left'     nowrap='true'><select
multiple><option><xsl:attribute                       name='value'><xsl:value-of
select=""data/Products/" + rs.Fields(x).Name  + """/></xsl:attribute><xsl:value-of
select=""data/Products/"        +          rs.Fields(x).Name                +
"""/></option></select></td></tr>")
```
SPAN

```
        txtstream.WriteLine("<td   align='left' nowrap='true'><span><xsl:value-
of select=""data/Products/" + rs.Fields(x).Name  + """/></span></td></tr>")
```

TEXTAREA

```
        txtstream.WriteLine("<td                                   align='left'
nowrap='true'><textarea><xsl:value-of          select=""data/Products/"       +
rs.Fields(x).Name  + """/></textarea></td></tr>")
```

TEXTBOX

```
        txtstream.WriteLine("<td          align='left'     nowrap='true'><input
type='text'><xsl:attribute  name=""value""><xsl:value-of select=""data/Products/"
+ rs.Fields(x).Name  + """/></xsl:attribute></input></td></tr>")
```

MULTI LINE VERTICAL TABLES

```
    txtstream.WriteLine("<table        style='border:Double;border-width:1px;border-
color:navy;' rules=all frames=both cellpadding=2 cellspacing=2 Width=0>")


    for x = 0 to rs.Fields.count-1
        txtstream.WriteLine("<tr><th       align='left'     nowrap='true'>"      +
rs.Fields(x).Name + "</th>")
```

NONE

txtstream.WriteLine("<xsl:for-each   select=""data/Products""><td align='left' nowrap='true'><xsl:value-of   select=""""   +   rs.Fields(x).Name   +   """"/></td></xsl:for-each></tr>")

BUTTON

txtstream.WriteLine("<xsl:for-each   select=""data/Products""><td align='left' nowrap='true'><button style='width:100%;'><xsl:value-of select="""" + rs.Fields(x).Name + """"/></button></td></xsl:for-each></tr>")

COMBOBOX

txtstream.WriteLine("<xsl:for-each   select=""data/Products""><td align='left'   nowrap='true'><select><option><xsl:attribute name='value'><xsl:value-of   select=""""   +   rs.Fields(x).Name   + """"/></xsl:attribute><xsl:value-of select=""data/Products/" + rs.Fields(x).Name   + """"/></option></select></td></xsl:for-each></tr>")

DIV

txtstream.WriteLine("<xsl:for-each   select=""data/Products""><td align='left'   nowrap='true'> <xsl:value-of   select=""data/Products/"   + rs.Fields(x).Name + """"/> </td></xsl:for-each></tr>")

LINK

txtstream.WriteLine("<xsl:for-each   select=""data/Products""><td align='left' nowrap='true'><a href='" + rs.Fields(x).Value + "'><xsl:value-of select=""data/Products/"   +   rs.Fields(x).Name   +   """"/></a></td></xsl:for-each></tr>")

LISTBOX

txtstream.WriteLine("<xsl:for-each   select=""data/Products""><td align='left'   nowrap='true'><select   multiple><option><xsl:attribute name='value'><xsl:value-of select=""data/Products/"   +   rs.Fields(x).Name   + """"/></xsl:attribute><xsl:value-of select=""data/Products/" + rs.Fields(x).Name   + """"/></option></select></td></xsl:for-each></tr>")

SPAN

txtstream.WriteLine("<xsl:for-each   select=""data/Products""><td align='left'   nowrap='true'><xsl:value-of   select=""data/Products/"   + rs.Fields(x).Name + """"/></td></xsl:for-each></tr>")

TEXTAREA

txtstream.WriteLine("<xsl:for-each   select=""data/Products""><td align='left'   nowrap='true'><textarea><xsl:value-of   select=""data/Products/"   + rs.Fields(x).Name + """"/></textarea></td></xsl:for-each></tr>")

TEXTBOX

txtstream.WriteLine("<xsl:for-each   select=""data/Products""><td align='left'   nowrap='true'><input   type='text'><xsl:attribute name=""value""><xsl:value-of select=""data/Products/" + rs.Fields(x).Name   + """"/></xsl:attribute></input></td></xsl:for-each></tr>")

txtstream.WriteLine("</table>")
txtstream.WriteLine("</body>")
txtstream.WriteLine("</html>")
txtstream.WriteLine("</xsl:template>")
txtstream.WriteLine("</xsl:stylesheet>")
txtstream.Close()

STYLESHEETS

BELOW ARE SOME STYLESHEETS I'VE PUT TOGETHER THAT CAN BE MODIFIED BY YOU. They are just examples.

NONE

```
txtstream.WriteLine("<style type='text/css'>")
txtstream.WriteLine("th")
txtstream.WriteLine("{")
txtstream.WriteLine("    COLOR: white;")
txtstream.WriteLine("}")
txtstream.WriteLine("td")
txtstream.WriteLine("{")
txtstream.WriteLine("    COLOR: white;")
txtstream.WriteLine("}")
txtstream.WriteLine("</style>")
```

BLACK AND WHITE TEXT

```
txtstream.WriteLine("<style type='text/css'>")
txtstream.WriteLine("th")
txtstream.WriteLine("{")
txtstream.WriteLine("    COLOR: white;")
txtstream.WriteLine("    BACKGROUND-COLOR: black;")
```

```
txtstream.WriteLine("    FONT-FAMILY:font-family: Cambria, serif;")
txtstream.WriteLine("    FONT-SIZE: 12px;")
txtstream.WriteLine("    text-align: left;")
txtstream.WriteLine("    white-Space: nowrap;")
txtstream.WriteLine("}")
txtstream.WriteLine("td")
txtstream.WriteLine("{")
txtstream.WriteLine("    COLOR: white;")
txtstream.WriteLine("    BACKGROUND-COLOR: black;")
txtstream.WriteLine("    FONT-FAMILY: font-family: Cambria, serif;")
txtstream.WriteLine("    FONT-SIZE: 12px;")
txtstream.WriteLine("    text-align: left;")
txtstream.WriteLine("    white-Space: nowrap;")
txtstream.WriteLine("}")
txtstream.WriteLine("div")
txtstream.WriteLine("{")
txtstream.WriteLine("    COLOR: white;")
txtstream.WriteLine("    BACKGROUND-COLOR: black;")
txtstream.WriteLine("    FONT-FAMILY: font-family: Cambria, serif;")
txtstream.WriteLine("    FONT-SIZE: 10px;")
txtstream.WriteLine("    text-align: left;")
txtstream.WriteLine("    white-Space: nowrap;")
txtstream.WriteLine("}")
txtstream.WriteLine("span")
txtstream.WriteLine("{")
txtstream.WriteLine("    COLOR: white;")
txtstream.WriteLine("    BACKGROUND-COLOR: black;")
txtstream.WriteLine("    FONT-FAMILY: font-family: Cambria, serif;")
txtstream.WriteLine("    FONT-SIZE: 10px;")
txtstream.WriteLine("    text-align: left;")
txtstream.WriteLine("    white-Space: nowrap;")
txtstream.WriteLine("    display:inline-block;")
txtstream.WriteLine("    width: 100%;")
txtstream.WriteLine("}")
txtstream.WriteLine("textarea")
```

```
txtstream.WriteLine("{")
txtstream.WriteLine("   COLOR: white;")
txtstream.WriteLine("   BACKGROUND-COLOR: black;")
txtstream.WriteLine("   FONT-FAMILY: font-family: Cambria, serif;")
txtstream.WriteLine("   FONT-SIZE: 10px;")
txtstream.WriteLine("   text-align: left;")
txtstream.WriteLine("   white-Space: nowrap;")
txtstream.WriteLine("   width: 100%;")
txtstream.WriteLine("}")
txtstream.WriteLine("select")
txtstream.WriteLine("{")
txtstream.WriteLine("   COLOR: white;")
txtstream.WriteLine("   BACKGROUND-COLOR: black;")
txtstream.WriteLine("   FONT-FAMILY: font-family: Cambria, serif;")
txtstream.WriteLine("   FONT-SIZE: 10px;")
txtstream.WriteLine("   text-align: left;")
txtstream.WriteLine("   white-Space: nowrap;")
txtstream.WriteLine("   width: 100%;")
txtstream.WriteLine("}")
txtstream.WriteLine("input")
txtstream.WriteLine("{")
txtstream.WriteLine("   COLOR: white;")
txtstream.WriteLine("   BACKGROUND-COLOR: black;")
txtstream.WriteLine("   FONT-FAMILY: font-family: Cambria, serif;")
txtstream.WriteLine("   FONT-SIZE: 12px;")
txtstream.WriteLine("   text-align: left;")
txtstream.WriteLine("   display:table-cell;")
txtstream.WriteLine("   white-Space: nowrap;")
txtstream.WriteLine("}")
txtstream.WriteLine("h1 {")
txtstream.WriteLine("color: antiquewhite;")
txtstream.WriteLine("text-shadow: 1px 1px 1px black;")
txtstream.WriteLine("padding: 3px;")
txtstream.WriteLine("text-align: center;")
```

```
txtstream.WriteLine("box-shadow: in2px 2px 5px rgba(0,0,0,0.5), in-
2px -2px 5px rgba(255,255,255,0.5);")
txtstream.WriteLine("}")
txtstream.WriteLine("</style>")
```

```
txtstream.WriteLine("<style type='text/css'>")
txtstream.WriteLine("th")
txtstream.WriteLine("{")
txtstream.WriteLine("   COLOR: darkred;")
txtstream.WriteLine("   BACKGROUND-COLOR: #eeeeee;")
txtstream.WriteLine("   FONT-FAMILY:font-family: Cambria, serif;")
txtstream.WriteLine("   FONT-SIZE: 12px;")
txtstream.WriteLine("   text-align: left;")
txtstream.WriteLine("   white-Space: nowrap;")
txtstream.WriteLine("}")
txtstream.WriteLine("td")
txtstream.WriteLine("{")
txtstream.WriteLine("   COLOR: navy;")
txtstream.WriteLine("   BACKGROUND-COLOR: #eeeeee;")
txtstream.WriteLine("   FONT-FAMILY: font-family: Cambria, serif;")
txtstream.WriteLine("   FONT-SIZE: 12px;")
txtstream.WriteLine("   text-align: left;")
txtstream.WriteLine("   white-Space: nowrap;")
txtstream.WriteLine("}")
txtstream.WriteLine("div")
txtstream.WriteLine("{")
txtstream.WriteLine("   COLOR: white;")
txtstream.WriteLine("   BACKGROUND-COLOR: navy;")
txtstream.WriteLine("   FONT-FAMILY: font-family: Cambria, serif;")
txtstream.WriteLine("   FONT-SIZE: 10px;")
txtstream.WriteLine("   text-align: left;")
txtstream.WriteLine("   white-Space: nowrap;")
txtstream.WriteLine("}")
txtstream.WriteLine("span")
```

```
txtstream.WriteLine("{")
txtstream.WriteLine("    COLOR: white;")
txtstream.WriteLine("    BACKGROUND-COLOR: navy;")
txtstream.WriteLine("    FONT-FAMILY: font-family: Cambria, serif;")
txtstream.WriteLine("    FONT-SIZE: 10px;")
txtstream.WriteLine("    text-align: left;")
txtstream.WriteLine("    white-Space: nowrap;")
txtstream.WriteLine("    display:inline-block;")
txtstream.WriteLine("    width: 100%;")
txtstream.WriteLine("}")
txtstream.WriteLine("textarea")
txtstream.WriteLine("{")
txtstream.WriteLine("    COLOR: white;")
txtstream.WriteLine("    BACKGROUND-COLOR: navy;")
txtstream.WriteLine("    FONT-FAMILY: font-family: Cambria, serif;")
txtstream.WriteLine("    FONT-SIZE: 10px;")
txtstream.WriteLine("    text-align: left;")
txtstream.WriteLine("    white-Space: nowrap;")
txtstream.WriteLine("    width: 100%;")
txtstream.WriteLine("}")
txtstream.WriteLine("select")
txtstream.WriteLine("{")
txtstream.WriteLine("    COLOR: white;")
txtstream.WriteLine("    BACKGROUND-COLOR: navy;")
txtstream.WriteLine("    FONT-FAMILY: font-family: Cambria, serif;")
txtstream.WriteLine("    FONT-SIZE: 10px;")
txtstream.WriteLine("    text-align: left;")
txtstream.WriteLine("    white-Space: nowrap;")
txtstream.WriteLine("    width: 100%;")
txtstream.WriteLine("}")
txtstream.WriteLine("input")
txtstream.WriteLine("{")
txtstream.WriteLine("    COLOR: white;")
txtstream.WriteLine("    BACKGROUND-COLOR: navy;")
txtstream.WriteLine("    FONT-FAMILY: font-family: Cambria, serif;")
```

```
txtstream.WriteLine("   FONT-SIZE: 12px;")
txtstream.WriteLine("   text-align: left;")
txtstream.WriteLine("   display:table-cell;")
txtstream.WriteLine("   white-Space: nowrap;")
txtstream.WriteLine("}")
txtstream.WriteLine("h1 {")
txtstream.WriteLine("color: antiquewhite;")
txtstream.WriteLine("text-shadow: 1px 1px 1px black;")
txtstream.WriteLine("padding: 3px;")
txtstream.WriteLine("text-align: center;")
txtstream.WriteLine("box-shadow: in2px 2px 5px rgba(0,0,0,0.5), in-2px -2px 5px rgba(255,255,255,0.5);")
txtstream.WriteLine("}")
txtstream.WriteLine("</style>")
```

OSCILLATING ROW COLORS

```
txtstream.WriteLine("<style>")
txtstream.WriteLine("th")
txtstream.WriteLine("{")
txtstream.WriteLine("   COLOR: white;")
txtstream.WriteLine("   BACKGROUND-COLOR: navy;")
txtstream.WriteLine("   FONT-FAMILY:font-family: Cambria, serif;")
txtstream.WriteLine("   FONT-SIZE: 12px;")
txtstream.WriteLine("   text-align: left;")
txtstream.WriteLine("   white-Space: nowrap;")
txtstream.WriteLine("}")
txtstream.WriteLine("td")
txtstream.WriteLine("{")
txtstream.WriteLine("   COLOR: navy;")
txtstream.WriteLine("   FONT-FAMILY: font-family: Cambria, serif;")
txtstream.WriteLine("   FONT-SIZE: 12px;")
txtstream.WriteLine("   text-align: left;")
```

```
txtstream.WriteLine("    white-Space: nowrap;")
txtstream.WriteLine("}")
txtstream.WriteLine("div")
txtstream.WriteLine("{")
txtstream.WriteLine("    COLOR: navy;")
txtstream.WriteLine("    FONT-FAMILY: font-family: Cambria, serif;")
txtstream.WriteLine("    FONT-SIZE: 12px;")
txtstream.WriteLine("    text-align: left;")
txtstream.WriteLine("    white-Space: nowrap;")
txtstream.WriteLine("}")
txtstream.WriteLine("span")
txtstream.WriteLine("{")
txtstream.WriteLine("    COLOR: navy;")
txtstream.WriteLine("    FONT-FAMILY: font-family: Cambria, serif;")
txtstream.WriteLine("    FONT-SIZE: 12px;")
txtstream.WriteLine("    text-align: left;")
txtstream.WriteLine("    white-Space: nowrap;")
txtstream.WriteLine("    width: 100%;")
txtstream.WriteLine("}")
txtstream.WriteLine("textarea")
txtstream.WriteLine("{")
txtstream.WriteLine("    COLOR: navy;")
txtstream.WriteLine("    FONT-FAMILY: font-family: Cambria, serif;")
txtstream.WriteLine("    FONT-SIZE: 12px;")
txtstream.WriteLine("    text-align: left;")
txtstream.WriteLine("    white-Space: nowrap;")
txtstream.WriteLine("    display:inline-block;")
txtstream.WriteLine("    width: 100%;")
txtstream.WriteLine("}")
txtstream.WriteLine("select")
txtstream.WriteLine("{")
txtstream.WriteLine("    COLOR: navy;")
txtstream.WriteLine("    FONT-FAMILY: font-family: Cambria, serif;")
txtstream.WriteLine("    FONT-SIZE: 10px;")
txtstream.WriteLine("    text-align: left;")
```

```
txtstream.WriteLine("    white-Space: nowrap;")
txtstream.WriteLine("    display:inline-block;")
txtstream.WriteLine("    width: 100%;")
txtstream.WriteLine("}")
txtstream.WriteLine("input")
txtstream.WriteLine("{")
txtstream.WriteLine("    COLOR: navy;")
txtstream.WriteLine("    FONT-FAMILY: font-family: Cambria, serif;")
txtstream.WriteLine("    FONT-SIZE: 12px;")
txtstream.WriteLine("    text-align: left;")
txtstream.WriteLine("    display:table-cell;")
txtstream.WriteLine("    white-Space: nowrap;")
txtstream.WriteLine("}")
txtstream.WriteLine("h1 {")
txtstream.WriteLine("color: antiquewhite;")
txtstream.WriteLine("text-shadow: 1px 1px 1px black;")
txtstream.WriteLine("padding: 3px;")
txtstream.WriteLine("text-align: center;")
txtstream.WriteLine("box-shadow: in2px 2px 5px rgba(0,0,0,0.5), in-2px -2px 5px rgba(255,255,255,0.5);")
txtstream.WriteLine("}")
txtstream.WriteLine("tr:nth-child(even){background-color:#f2f2f2;}")
txtstream.WriteLine("tr:nth-child(odd){background-color:#cccccc; color:#f2f2f2;}")
txtstream.WriteLine("</style>")
```

GHOST DECORATED

```
txtstream.WriteLine("<style type='text/css'>")
txtstream.WriteLine("th")
txtstream.WriteLine("{")
txtstream.WriteLine("    COLOR: black;")
txtstream.WriteLine("    BACKGROUND-COLOR: white;")
txtstream.WriteLine("    FONT-FAMILY:font-family: Cambria, serif;")
txtstream.WriteLine("    FONT-SIZE: 12px;")
```

```
txtstream.WriteLine("    text-align: left;")
txtstream.WriteLine("    white-Space: nowrap;")
txtstream.WriteLine("}")
txtstream.WriteLine("td")
txtstream.WriteLine("{")
txtstream.WriteLine("    COLOR: black;")
txtstream.WriteLine("    BACKGROUND-COLOR: white;")
txtstream.WriteLine("    FONT-FAMILY: font-family: Cambria, serif;")
txtstream.WriteLine("    FONT-SIZE: 12px;")
txtstream.WriteLine("    text-align: left;")
txtstream.WriteLine("    white-Space: nowrap;")
txtstream.WriteLine("}")
txtstream.WriteLine("div")
txtstream.WriteLine("{")
txtstream.WriteLine("    COLOR: black;")
txtstream.WriteLine("    BACKGROUND-COLOR: white;")
txtstream.WriteLine("    FONT-FAMILY: font-family: Cambria, serif;")
txtstream.WriteLine("    FONT-SIZE: 10px;")
txtstream.WriteLine("    text-align: left;")
txtstream.WriteLine("    white-Space: nowrap;")
txtstream.WriteLine("}")
txtstream.WriteLine("span")
txtstream.WriteLine("{")
txtstream.WriteLine("    COLOR: black;")
txtstream.WriteLine("    BACKGROUND-COLOR: white;")
txtstream.WriteLine("    FONT-FAMILY: font-family: Cambria, serif;")
txtstream.WriteLine("    FONT-SIZE: 10px;")
txtstream.WriteLine("    text-align: left;")
txtstream.WriteLine("    white-Space: nowrap;")
txtstream.WriteLine("    display:inline-block;")
txtstream.WriteLine("    width: 100%;")
txtstream.WriteLine("}")
txtstream.WriteLine("textarea")
txtstream.WriteLine("{")
txtstream.WriteLine("    COLOR: black;")
```

```
txtstream.WriteLine("    BACKGROUND-COLOR: white;")
txtstream.WriteLine("    FONT-FAMILY: font-family: Cambria, serif;")
txtstream.WriteLine("    FONT-SIZE: 10px;")
txtstream.WriteLine("    text-align: left;")
txtstream.WriteLine("    white-Space: nowrap;")
txtstream.WriteLine("    width: 100%;")
txtstream.WriteLine("}")
txtstream.WriteLine("select")
txtstream.WriteLine("{")
txtstream.WriteLine("    COLOR: black;")
txtstream.WriteLine("    BACKGROUND-COLOR: white;")
txtstream.WriteLine("    FONT-FAMILY: font-family: Cambria, serif;")
txtstream.WriteLine("    FONT-SIZE: 10px;")
txtstream.WriteLine("    text-align: left;")
txtstream.WriteLine("    white-Space: nowrap;")
txtstream.WriteLine("    width: 100%;")
txtstream.WriteLine("}")
txtstream.WriteLine("input")
txtstream.WriteLine("{")
txtstream.WriteLine("    COLOR: black;")
txtstream.WriteLine("    BACKGROUND-COLOR: white;")
txtstream.WriteLine("    FONT-FAMILY: font-family: Cambria, serif;")
txtstream.WriteLine("    FONT-SIZE: 12px;")
txtstream.WriteLine("    text-align: left;")
txtstream.WriteLine("    display:table-cell;")
txtstream.WriteLine("    white-Space: nowrap;")
txtstream.WriteLine("}")
txtstream.WriteLine("h1 {")
txtstream.WriteLine("color: antiquewhite;")
txtstream.WriteLine("text-shadow: 1px 1px 1px black;")
txtstream.WriteLine("padding: 3px;")
txtstream.WriteLine("text-align: center;")
txtstream.WriteLine("box-shadow: in2px 2px 5px rgba(0,0,0,0.5), in-2px -2px 5px rgba(255,255,255,0.5);")
txtstream.WriteLine("}")
```

```
txtstream.WriteLine("</style>")
```

3D

```
txtstream.WriteLine("<style type='text/css'>")
txtstream.WriteLine("body")
txtstream.WriteLine("{")
txtstream.WriteLine("   PADDING-RIGHT: 0px;")
txtstream.WriteLine("   PADDING-LEFT: 0px;")
txtstream.WriteLine("   PADDING-BOTTOM: 0px;")
txtstream.WriteLine("   MARGIN: 0px;")
txtstream.WriteLine("   COLOR: #333;")
txtstream.WriteLine("   PADDING-TOP: 0px;")
txtstream.WriteLine("    FONT-FAMILY: verdana, arial, helvetica, sans-
serif;")
txtstream.WriteLine("}")
txtstream.WriteLine("table")
txtstream.WriteLine("{")
txtstream.WriteLine("   BORDER-RIGHT: #999999 3px solid;")
txtstream.WriteLine("   PADDING-RIGHT: 6px;")
txtstream.WriteLine("   PADDING-LEFT: 6px;")
txtstream.WriteLine("   FONT-WEIGHT: Bold;")
txtstream.WriteLine("   FONT-SIZE: 14px;")
txtstream.WriteLine("   PADDING-BOTTOM: 6px;")
txtstream.WriteLine("   COLOR: Peru;")
txtstream.WriteLine("   LINE-HEIGHT: 14px;")
txtstream.WriteLine("   PADDING-TOP: 6px;")
txtstream.WriteLine("   BORDER-BOTTOM: #999 1px solid;")
txtstream.WriteLine("   BACKGROUND-COLOR: #eeeeee;")
txtstream.WriteLine("    FONT-FAMILY: verdana, arial, helvetica, sans-
serif;")
txtstream.WriteLine("   FONT-SIZE: 12px;")
txtstream.WriteLine("}")
txtstream.WriteLine("th")
```

```
txtstream.WriteLine("{")
txtstream.WriteLine("    BORDER-RIGHT: #999999 3px solid;")
txtstream.WriteLine("    PADDING-RIGHT: 6px;")
txtstream.WriteLine("    PADDING-LEFT: 6px;")
txtstream.WriteLine("    FONT-WEIGHT: Bold;")
txtstream.WriteLine("    FONT-SIZE: 14px;")
txtstream.WriteLine("    PADDING-BOTTOM: 6px;")
txtstream.WriteLine("    COLOR: darkred;")
txtstream.WriteLine("    LINE-HEIGHT: 14px;")
txtstream.WriteLine("    PADDING-TOP: 6px;")
txtstream.WriteLine("    BORDER-BOTTOM: #999 1px solid;")
txtstream.WriteLine("    BACKGROUND-COLOR: #eeeeee;")
txtstream.WriteLine("    FONT-FAMILY:font-family: Cambria, serif;")
txtstream.WriteLine("    FONT-SIZE: 12px;")
txtstream.WriteLine("    text-align: left;")
txtstream.WriteLine("    white-Space: nowrap;")
txtstream.WriteLine("}")
txtstream.WriteLine(".th")
txtstream.WriteLine("{")
txtstream.WriteLine("    BORDER-RIGHT: #999999 2px solid;")
txtstream.WriteLine("    PADDING-RIGHT: 6px;")
txtstream.WriteLine("    PADDING-LEFT: 6px;")
txtstream.WriteLine("    FONT-WEIGHT: Bold;")
txtstream.WriteLine("    PADDING-BOTTOM: 6px;")
txtstream.WriteLine("    COLOR: black;")
txtstream.WriteLine("    PADDING-TOP: 6px;")
txtstream.WriteLine("    BORDER-BOTTOM: #999 2px solid;")
txtstream.WriteLine("    BACKGROUND-COLOR: #eeeeee;")
txtstream.WriteLine("    FONT-FAMILY: font-family: Cambria, serif;")
txtstream.WriteLine("    FONT-SIZE: 10px;")
txtstream.WriteLine("    text-align: right;")
txtstream.WriteLine("    white-Space: nowrap;")
txtstream.WriteLine("}")
txtstream.WriteLine("td")
txtstream.WriteLine("{")
```

```
txtstream.WriteLine("    BORDER-RIGHT: #999999 3px solid;")
txtstream.WriteLine("    PADDING-RIGHT: 6px;")
txtstream.WriteLine("    PADDING-LEFT: 6px;")
txtstream.WriteLine("    FONT-WEIGHT: Normal;")
txtstream.WriteLine("    PADDING-BOTTOM: 6px;")
txtstream.WriteLine("    COLOR: navy;")
txtstream.WriteLine("    LINE-HEIGHT: 14px;")
txtstream.WriteLine("    PADDING-TOP: 6px;")
txtstream.WriteLine("    BORDER-BOTTOM: #999 1px solid;")
txtstream.WriteLine("    BACKGROUND-COLOR: #eeeeee;")
txtstream.WriteLine("    FONT-FAMILY: font-family: Cambria, serif;")
txtstream.WriteLine("    FONT-SIZE: 12px;")
txtstream.WriteLine("    text-align: left;")
txtstream.WriteLine("    white-Space: nowrap;")
txtstream.WriteLine("}")
txtstream.WriteLine("div")
txtstream.WriteLine("{")
txtstream.WriteLine("    BORDER-RIGHT: #999999 3px solid;")
txtstream.WriteLine("    PADDING-RIGHT: 6px;")
txtstream.WriteLine("    PADDING-LEFT: 6px;")
txtstream.WriteLine("    FONT-WEIGHT: Normal;")
txtstream.WriteLine("    PADDING-BOTTOM: 6px;")
txtstream.WriteLine("    COLOR: white;")
txtstream.WriteLine("    PADDING-TOP: 6px;")
txtstream.WriteLine("    BORDER-BOTTOM: #999 1px solid;")
txtstream.WriteLine("    BACKGROUND-COLOR: navy;")
txtstream.WriteLine("    FONT-FAMILY: font-family: Cambria, serif;")
txtstream.WriteLine("    FONT-SIZE: 10px;")
txtstream.WriteLine("    text-align: left;")
txtstream.WriteLine("    white-Space: nowrap;")
txtstream.WriteLine("}")
txtstream.WriteLine("span")
txtstream.WriteLine("{")
txtstream.WriteLine("    BORDER-RIGHT: #999999 3px solid;")
txtstream.WriteLine("    PADDING-RIGHT: 3px;")
```

```
txtstream.WriteLine("    PADDING-LEFT: 3px;")
txtstream.WriteLine("    FONT-WEIGHT: Normal;")
txtstream.WriteLine("    PADDING-BOTTOM: 3px;")
txtstream.WriteLine("    COLOR: white;")
txtstream.WriteLine("    PADDING-TOP: 3px;")
txtstream.WriteLine("    BORDER-BOTTOM: #999 1px solid;")
txtstream.WriteLine("    BACKGROUND-COLOR: navy;")
txtstream.WriteLine("    FONT-FAMILY: font-family: Cambria, serif;")
txtstream.WriteLine("    FONT-SIZE: 10px;")
txtstream.WriteLine("    text-align: left;")
txtstream.WriteLine("    white-Space: nowrap;")
txtstream.WriteLine("    display:inline-block;")
txtstream.WriteLine("    width: 100%;")
txtstream.WriteLine("}")
txtstream.WriteLine("textarea")
txtstream.WriteLine("{")
txtstream.WriteLine("    BORDER-RIGHT: #999999 3px solid;")
txtstream.WriteLine("    PADDING-RIGHT: 3px;")
txtstream.WriteLine("    PADDING-LEFT: 3px;")
txtstream.WriteLine("    FONT-WEIGHT: Normal;")
txtstream.WriteLine("    PADDING-BOTTOM: 3px;")
txtstream.WriteLine("    COLOR: white;")
txtstream.WriteLine("    PADDING-TOP: 3px;")
txtstream.WriteLine("    BORDER-BOTTOM: #999 1px solid;")
txtstream.WriteLine("    BACKGROUND-COLOR: navy;")
txtstream.WriteLine("    FONT-FAMILY: font-family: Cambria, serif;")
txtstream.WriteLine("    FONT-SIZE: 10px;")
txtstream.WriteLine("    text-align: left;")
txtstream.WriteLine("    white-Space: nowrap;")
txtstream.WriteLine("    width: 100%;")
txtstream.WriteLine("}")
txtstream.WriteLine("select")
txtstream.WriteLine("{")
txtstream.WriteLine("    BORDER-RIGHT: #999999 3px solid;")
txtstream.WriteLine("    PADDING-RIGHT: 6px;")
```

```
txtstream.WriteLine("    PADDING-LEFT: 6px;")
txtstream.WriteLine("    FONT-WEIGHT: Normal;")
txtstream.WriteLine("    PADDING-BOTTOM: 6px;")
txtstream.WriteLine("    COLOR: white;")
txtstream.WriteLine("    PADDING-TOP: 6px;")
txtstream.WriteLine("    BORDER-BOTTOM: #999 1px solid;")
txtstream.WriteLine("    BACKGROUND-COLOR: navy;")
txtstream.WriteLine("    FONT-FAMILY: font-family: Cambria, serif;")
txtstream.WriteLine("    FONT-SIZE: 10px;")
txtstream.WriteLine("    text-align: left;")
txtstream.WriteLine("    white-Space: nowrap;")
txtstream.WriteLine("    width: 100%;")
txtstream.WriteLine("}")
txtstream.WriteLine("input")
txtstream.WriteLine("{")
txtstream.WriteLine("    BORDER-RIGHT: #999999 3px solid;")
txtstream.WriteLine("    PADDING-RIGHT: 3px;")
txtstream.WriteLine("    PADDING-LEFT: 3px;")
txtstream.WriteLine("    FONT-WEIGHT: Bold;")
txtstream.WriteLine("    PADDING-BOTTOM: 3px;")
txtstream.WriteLine("    COLOR: white;")
txtstream.WriteLine("    PADDING-TOP: 3px;")
txtstream.WriteLine("    BORDER-BOTTOM: #999 1px solid;")
txtstream.WriteLine("    BACKGROUND-COLOR: navy;")
txtstream.WriteLine("    FONT-FAMILY: font-family: Cambria, serif;")
txtstream.WriteLine("    FONT-SIZE: 12px;")
txtstream.WriteLine("    text-align: left;")
txtstream.WriteLine("    display:table-cell;")
txtstream.WriteLine("    white-Space: nowrap;")
txtstream.WriteLine("    width: 100%;")
txtstream.WriteLine("}")
txtstream.WriteLine("h1 {")
txtstream.WriteLine("color: antiquewhite;")
txtstream.WriteLine("text-shadow: 1px 1px 1px black;")
txtstream.WriteLine("padding: 3px;")
```

```
txtstream.WriteLine("text-align: center;")
txtstream.WriteLine("box-shadow: in2px 2px 5px rgba(0,0,0,0.5), in-
2px -2px 5px rgba(255,255,255,0.5);")
txtstream.WriteLine("}")
txtstream.WriteLine("</style>")
```

SHADOW BOX

```
txtstream.WriteLine("<style type='text/css'>")
txtstream.WriteLine("body")
txtstream.WriteLine("{")
txtstream.WriteLine("    PADDING-RIGHT: 0px;")
txtstream.WriteLine("    PADDING-LEFT: 0px;")
txtstream.WriteLine("    PADDING-BOTTOM: 0px;")
txtstream.WriteLine("    MARGIN: 0px;")
txtstream.WriteLine("    COLOR: #333;")
txtstream.WriteLine("    PADDING-TOP: 0px;")
txtstream.WriteLine("    FONT-FAMILY: verdana, arial, helvetica, sans-
serif;")
txtstream.WriteLine("}")
txtstream.WriteLine("table")
txtstream.WriteLine("{")
txtstream.WriteLine("    BORDER-RIGHT: #999999 1px solid;")
txtstream.WriteLine("    PADDING-RIGHT: 1px;")
txtstream.WriteLine("    PADDING-LEFT: 1px;")
txtstream.WriteLine("    PADDING-BOTTOM: 1px;")
txtstream.WriteLine("    LINE-HEIGHT: 8px;")
txtstream.WriteLine("    PADDING-TOP: 1px;")
txtstream.WriteLine("    BORDER-BOTTOM: #999 1px solid;")
txtstream.WriteLine("    BACKGROUND-COLOR: #eeeeee;")
txtstream.WriteLine("
filter:progid:DXImageTransform.Microsoft.Shadow(color='silver',
Direction=135, Strength=16)")
txtstream.WriteLine("}")
txtstream.WriteLine("th")
```

```
txtstream.WriteLine("{")
txtstream.WriteLine("    BORDER-RIGHT: #999999 3px solid;")
txtstream.WriteLine("    PADDING-RIGHT: 6px;")
txtstream.WriteLine("    PADDING-LEFT: 6px;")
txtstream.WriteLine("    FONT-WEIGHT: Bold;")
txtstream.WriteLine("    FONT-SIZE: 14px;")
txtstream.WriteLine("    PADDING-BOTTOM: 6px;")
txtstream.WriteLine("    COLOR: darkred;")
txtstream.WriteLine("    LINE-HEIGHT: 14px;")
txtstream.WriteLine("    PADDING-TOP: 6px;")
txtstream.WriteLine("    BORDER-BOTTOM: #999 1px solid;")
txtstream.WriteLine("    BACKGROUND-COLOR: #eeeeee;")
txtstream.WriteLine("    FONT-FAMILY:font-family: Cambria, serif;")
txtstream.WriteLine("    FONT-SIZE: 12px;")
txtstream.WriteLine("    text-align: left;")
txtstream.WriteLine("    white-Space: nowrap;")
txtstream.WriteLine("}")
txtstream.WriteLine(".th")
txtstream.WriteLine("{")
txtstream.WriteLine("    BORDER-RIGHT: #999999 2px solid;")
txtstream.WriteLine("    PADDING-RIGHT: 6px;")
txtstream.WriteLine("    PADDING-LEFT: 6px;")
txtstream.WriteLine("    FONT-WEIGHT: Bold;")
txtstream.WriteLine("    PADDING-BOTTOM: 6px;")
txtstream.WriteLine("    COLOR: black;")
txtstream.WriteLine("    PADDING-TOP: 6px;")
txtstream.WriteLine("    BORDER-BOTTOM: #999 2px solid;")
txtstream.WriteLine("    BACKGROUND-COLOR: #eeeeee;")
txtstream.WriteLine("    FONT-FAMILY: font-family: Cambria, serif;")
txtstream.WriteLine("    FONT-SIZE: 10px;")
txtstream.WriteLine("    text-align: right;")
txtstream.WriteLine("    white-Space: nowrap;")
txtstream.WriteLine("}")
txtstream.WriteLine("td")
txtstream.WriteLine("{")
```

```
txtstream.WriteLine("    BORDER-RIGHT: #999999 3px solid;")
txtstream.WriteLine("    PADDING-RIGHT: 6px;")
txtstream.WriteLine("    PADDING-LEFT: 6px;")
txtstream.WriteLine("    FONT-WEIGHT: Normal;")
txtstream.WriteLine("    PADDING-BOTTOM: 6px;")
txtstream.WriteLine("    COLOR: navy;")
txtstream.WriteLine("    LINE-HEIGHT: 14px;")
txtstream.WriteLine("    PADDING-TOP: 6px;")
txtstream.WriteLine("    BORDER-BOTTOM: #999 1px solid;")
txtstream.WriteLine("    BACKGROUND-COLOR: #eeeeee;")
txtstream.WriteLine("    FONT-FAMILY: font-family: Cambria, serif;")
txtstream.WriteLine("    FONT-SIZE: 12px;")
txtstream.WriteLine("    text-align: left;")
txtstream.WriteLine("    white-Space: nowrap;")
txtstream.WriteLine("}")
txtstream.WriteLine("div")
txtstream.WriteLine("{")
txtstream.WriteLine("    BORDER-RIGHT: #999999 3px solid;")
txtstream.WriteLine("    PADDING-RIGHT: 6px;")
txtstream.WriteLine("    PADDING-LEFT: 6px;")
txtstream.WriteLine("    FONT-WEIGHT: Normal;")
txtstream.WriteLine("    PADDING-BOTTOM: 6px;")
txtstream.WriteLine("    COLOR: white;")
txtstream.WriteLine("    PADDING-TOP: 6px;")
txtstream.WriteLine("    BORDER-BOTTOM: #999 1px solid;")
txtstream.WriteLine("    BACKGROUND-COLOR: navy;")
txtstream.WriteLine("    FONT-FAMILY: font-family: Cambria, serif;")
txtstream.WriteLine("    FONT-SIZE: 10px;")
txtstream.WriteLine("    text-align: left;")
txtstream.WriteLine("    white-Space: nowrap;")
txtstream.WriteLine("}")
txtstream.WriteLine("span")
txtstream.WriteLine("{")
txtstream.WriteLine("    BORDER-RIGHT: #999999 3px solid;")
txtstream.WriteLine("    PADDING-RIGHT: 3px;")
```

```
txtstream.WriteLine("    PADDING-LEFT: 3px;")
txtstream.WriteLine("    FONT-WEIGHT: Normal;")
txtstream.WriteLine("    PADDING-BOTTOM: 3px;")
txtstream.WriteLine("    COLOR: white;")
txtstream.WriteLine("    PADDING-TOP: 3px;")
txtstream.WriteLine("    BORDER-BOTTOM: #999 1px solid;")
txtstream.WriteLine("    BACKGROUND-COLOR: navy;")
txtstream.WriteLine("    FONT-FAMILY: font-family: Cambria, serif;")
txtstream.WriteLine("    FONT-SIZE: 10px;")
txtstream.WriteLine("    text-align: left;")
txtstream.WriteLine("    white-Space: nowrap;")
txtstream.WriteLine("    display:inline-block;")
txtstream.WriteLine("    width: 100%;")
txtstream.WriteLine("}")
txtstream.WriteLine("textarea")
txtstream.WriteLine("{")
txtstream.WriteLine("    BORDER-RIGHT: #999999 3px solid;")
txtstream.WriteLine("    PADDING-RIGHT: 3px;")
txtstream.WriteLine("    PADDING-LEFT: 3px;")
txtstream.WriteLine("    FONT-WEIGHT: Normal;")
txtstream.WriteLine("    PADDING-BOTTOM: 3px;")
txtstream.WriteLine("    COLOR: white;")
txtstream.WriteLine("    PADDING-TOP: 3px;")
txtstream.WriteLine("    BORDER-BOTTOM: #999 1px solid;")
txtstream.WriteLine("    BACKGROUND-COLOR: navy;")
txtstream.WriteLine("    FONT-FAMILY: font-family:Cambria, serif;")
txtstream.WriteLine("    FONT-SIZE: 10px;")
txtstream.WriteLine("    text-align: left;")
txtstream.WriteLine("    white-Space: nowrap;")
txtstream.WriteLine("    width: 100%;")
txtstream.WriteLine("}")
txtstream.WriteLine("select")
txtstream.WriteLine("{")
txtstream.WriteLine("    BORDER-RIGHT: #999999 3px solid;")
txtstream.WriteLine("    PADDING-RIGHT: 6px;")
```

```
txtstream.WriteLine("    PADDING-LEFT: 6px;")
txtstream.WriteLine("    FONT-WEIGHT: Normal;")
txtstream.WriteLine("    PADDING-BOTTOM: 6px;")
txtstream.WriteLine("    COLOR: white;")
txtstream.WriteLine("    PADDING-TOP: 6px;")
txtstream.WriteLine("    BORDER-BOTTOM: #999 1px solid;")
txtstream.WriteLine("    BACKGROUND-COLOR: navy;")
txtstream.WriteLine("    FONT-FAMILY: font-family:Cambria, serif;")
txtstream.WriteLine("    FONT-SIZE: 10px;")
txtstream.WriteLine("    text-align: left;")
txtstream.WriteLine("    white-Space: nowrap;")
txtstream.WriteLine("    width: 100%;")
txtstream.WriteLine("}")
txtstream.WriteLine("input")
txtstream.WriteLine("{")
txtstream.WriteLine("    BORDER-RIGHT: #999999 3px solid;")
txtstream.WriteLine("    PADDING-RIGHT: 3px;")
txtstream.WriteLine("    PADDING-LEFT: 3px;")
txtstream.WriteLine("    FONT-WEIGHT: Bold;")
txtstream.WriteLine("    PADDING-BOTTOM: 3px;")
txtstream.WriteLine("    COLOR: white;")
txtstream.WriteLine("    PADDING-TOP: 3px;")
txtstream.WriteLine("    BORDER-BOTTOM: #999 1px solid;")
txtstream.WriteLine("    BACKGROUND-COLOR: navy;")
txtstream.WriteLine("    FONT-FAMILY: font-family: Cambria, serif;")
txtstream.WriteLine("    FONT-SIZE: 12px;")
txtstream.WriteLine("    text-align: left;")
txtstream.WriteLine("    display: table-cell;")
txtstream.WriteLine("    white-Space: nowrap;")
txtstream.WriteLine("    width: 100%;")
txtstream.WriteLine("}")
txtstream.WriteLine("h1 {")
txtstream.WriteLine("color: antiquewhite;")
txtstream.WriteLine("text-shadow: 1px 1px 1px black;")
txtstream.WriteLine("padding: 3px;")
```

```
txtstream.WriteLine("text-align: center;")
txtstream.WriteLine("box-shadow: in2px 2px 5px rgba(0,0,0,0.5), in-
2px -2px 5px rgba(255,255,255,0.5);")
txtstream.WriteLine("}")
txtstream.WriteLine("</style>")
```

www.ingramcontent.com/pod-product-compliance
Lightning Source LLC
Chambersburg PA
CBHW070844070326
40690CB00009B/1695